Tom Farndon

Tom Farndon

The Greatest Speedway Rider of Them All

NORMAN JACOBS & JOHN CHAPLIN

The
History
Press

Also by Norman Jacobs

Speedway in East Anglia
Speedway in London
Speedway in the South East
Two Wimbledon Legends
Images of Sport: Norwich Speedway (with Mike Kemp)
Speedway's Classic Meetings (with Chris Broadbent)
Wembley Speedway: The Pre-War Years (with Peter Lipscomb)
75 Years of Eastbourne Speedway (with Ken Burnett)
70 Years of Rye House Speedway
Out of the Frying Pan: The Story of New Cross Speedway

Also by John Chaplin

Speedway: The Story of the World Championship
John Chaplin's Speedway Special: The Classic Legends
A Fistful Of Twistgrip
Ove Fundin: Speedway Superstar

First published 2010

The History Press
The Mill, Brimscombe Port
Stroud, Gloucestershire, GL5 2QG
www.thehistorypress.co.uk

British Library Cataloguing in Publication Data.
A catalogue record for this book is available from the British Library.

ISBN 978 0 7524 5140 4

Typesetting and origination by The History Press
Printed in Great Britain
Manufacturing managed by Jellyfish Print Solutions Ltd

We wish to dedicate this book to the memory of Tom Farndon, also to promoters Fred Mockford and Cecil Smith and all riders from the past who wore the colours of Coventry, Crystal Palace and New Cross. And to the great worldwide speedway family, now and in the future . . . may we continue 'Marching Along Together'!

'Tom Farndon showed (the crowds) Speedway Racing as only an expert can show it. He showed it them in his own style, which was unlike that of any other rider; he showed it them at its most spectacular and its most thrilling. And the people, although seeing something new, something they did not altogether understand, at once recognised in it the skill, the courage and the dashing sportsmanship of the boy they at once took to their hearts.'

Fred Mockford, promoter New Cross Speedway

About the Authors

NORMAN JACOBS

NORMAN JACOBS was named after a speedway rider, Norman Parker, the Wimbledon captain, so speedway has been in his blood since birth. Norman became well-known as a writer on local and family history from the 1970s onwards. As well as writing many books on the subject he also had many articles published in a wide variety of journals and magazines such as *Apollo, Local History Magazine, Essex Journal, Picture Postcard Monthly* and *Cockney Ancestor*. Between 1990 and 2005 he was editor of *Clacton Chronicle*, acclaimed the best local history journal in the country by *Local History Magazine*. In 1999 he persuaded Tempus Publishing to publish his (and their) first speedway book, *Speedway in East Anglia*. It was an immediate success, selling out in under a month and starting the recent boom in speedway publications. His second speedway book, *Speedway in London*, reached no. 3 in the *Sunday Times* Sports Books Chart.

The whole of his thirty-seven-year working life was at the British Museum and he is currently writing a book based on his experiences in the job.

JOHN CHAPLIN

JOHN CHAPLIN first saw speedway at Birmingham in 1946. He has had vast experience of reporting and commentating on the sport as a writer, author and broadcaster on radio and television. For more than fifty years he has contributed to publications throughout the world, principally the leading British speedway magazine, *Speedway Star*. He is a former Fleet Street journalist on the staff of the *Daily Mirror* and *Daily Mail* and was Deputy Editor of *UK Mail International*, the weekly international edition of the *Daily Mail*. He was also co-founder and editor of the acclaimed and highly successful periodical *Vintage Speedway Magazine*. His knowledge of the sport has been up close and personal through his eldest son Christopher who rode for Hackney and Rye House and was Anglia Junior Champion in 1983.

Contents

Foreword

by Betty Farndon

I was introduced to the Farndon family in 1951, after meeting Roy, Tom's son, at a local cycle speedway track. I was a big speedway fan and most of our courting was done at Brandon speedway watching such riders as Bob Fletcher, Derek Tailby, Lionel Levy, Johnnie Reason and Eddie 'Crusty' Pye, all riding for the Bees. We travelled around with Audrey, Roy's mother, supporting him when he was racing. I wasn't aware at the time of who his father was. Roy was a very good cycle speedway rider and rode for Radford Wasps and the Courthouse Cobras. He won the Bob Fletcher Trophy and quite a few cups. Our whole life was speedway at that time. Monday night it was racing practice; Wednesday night they were at home; Thursday night they rode away; Friday was the Brandon speedway supporters' club social evening where we always had a dance; and every Saturday night we used to queue up, miles and miles round Pool Meadow, to get the double-decker buses – the fare would have been about a shilling – which took thousands of us to Brandon for the speedway and we always used to stand on the back straight. All of us would go down to the pits to get that wonderful smell, and we knew all the riders.

I discovered the significance of the Farndon name because when Roy used to ride on the cycle speedway a lot of the riders used to be out to get him because of who he was. But he was always very good on a bike. His grandfather used to cut up old tyres to make a tread on the bottom of his shoe so that he wouldn't wear them out putting his foot down on the corners. I remember he wanted to put a little plaque on his bike with Tom Farndon Jnr on it, but his grandfather wouldn't let him. He said, 'You're not riding on your father's name, you're riding on your own.'

At about the same time he had his call-up papers for national service, a letter came from the Coventry promoter Charles Ochiltree asking him if he would like to have a trial for the Bees. However, his mother naturally wasn't very keen, so he never followed his father onto the track.

Roy Farndon in the RAF.

He went into the air force and signed on for five years, becoming an RAF Policeman. Roy eventually joined the police force and made it his career. He was a Detective Sergeant when he retired from the West Midlands force. He never wanted a higher office job, he wanted to be out and about catching villains.

Audrey remarried when Roy was five years old to a man named Ernie Taylor and they had two more children together. Roy really idolised his stepfather who treated him like one of his own. Ernie worked on aircraft during the war and was a fine sculptor in metal.

Audrey was sixty-two when she died in 1974. She always talked about Tom, especially about his father because his father was an old rogue. Tom's mother, Emily, the old gran, she was nice. She used to say to us she knew immediately when Roy was coming to visit her because he walked just like Tom. She could tell by his footsteps.

I'd like to say a special thank you to a very fine gentleman, Eric Dillon, who lived in Deptford and was a dedicated Tom Farndon fan. Every year on the anniversary of Tom's death he put a memorial message in the *Daily Telegraph*. He contacted the family through 'The Old Codgers' who used to have a page in the *Daily Mirror* and we met at Tom's grave in St Paul's cemetery. When he died he left Roy three wonderful albums which he had lovingly compiled and an audio tape of the memorial service held at the New Cross track. He had a room in his house completely dedicated to Tom and New Cross speedway. Eventually the albums will be passed on to the family.

Unfortunately Roy passed away in May 2008 and I know he would have been so proud to think a biography of his father was being written and for him to be remembered in this way. My thanks go to Norman Jacobs and John Chaplin for writing it, and also thanks to John for all the photographs he found and e-mailed to me.

There is still a Tom Farndon – one of my grandsons who lives in New York. Very recently I gave him a propelling pencil his great grandfather was presented with at Crystal Palace in 1933 by the supporters' club – it still works – and I also gave him one of the plaques presented to Tom for appearing in Test matches against Australia. Roy and I had three children, two boys and a girl, Martin, Keith and Anne. But no one in the family is likely to be a speedway rider.

Betty Farndon, Moraira, Alicante, Spain, August 2009

Tom Farndon.

1

A NIGHT LIKE NO OTHER

It was a star-studded meeting, but the biggest name on the programme was the idol of the Old Kent Road fans, Tom Farndon.

For the residents of Ilderton Road, SE15, in the London Borough of Southwark, it was just another Wednesday night. Over the best part of a year and a half the occupants of the curving row of little terraced houses backing onto New Cross Stadium had become accustomed to the weekly rumble of high-powered motorcycle engines being warmed up on the other side of their back garden fences. The New Cross speedway pits were practically in their back gardens, and no one seemed to complain about the noise. There was plenty of it, ever since pioneer promoters Freddie Mockford and Cecil Smith, proprietors of London Motor Sports Ltd, had moved their dirt-track enterprise the previous year from the picturesque Crystal Palace into the neat little arena south of the river.

Now, every week in the summer, the crowds swarmed into the area in their thousands, alighting from the trams on the Old Kent Road, decked out in the orange and black colours of the New Cross speedway team, waving their banners, shouting their war cries and the names of their new-found leather-clad heroes. As their enthusiasm swept them along Ilderton Road, and they turned right into Hornshay Street, it was like a regular good natured carnival. It generated a build-up of excitement, which went on mounting until the familiar New Cross signature tune, 'Marching Along Together', began to crackle out from the trackside loudspeakers. It was the moment they knew the real thrills were about to begin. What they could not possibly know was that fate had decreed that this night, Wednesday 28 August 1935, would be like no other – before or since.

There was world class speedway every week night in London: at Wimbledon on Mondays, West Ham on Tuesdays, New Cross on Wednesdays, Wembley on Thursdays and Harringay on Fridays. On Saturday nights the show moved out of town to Manchester. The Aces at Belle Vue seemed to hold most of speedway's winning cards. They had been National League champions for the past two years in succession and looked like making it three in a row.

New Cross were lying second in the league at the time. Their most serious challengers were the Harringay side from North London, that night's visitors. The Tigers were on a winning streak, led by Jack Parker, holder of the Star Championship, who was the nearest the sport had then to a World Champion. The team was made up of practically all internationals: Jack's brother Norman, multiple Star finalist Les Wotton, former Wembley star Jack Ormston plus England regulars Phil Bishop and Bill Pitcher, with the very experienced Billy Dallison at reserve. New Cross, led by former British Champion and Australian international Ron Johnson, were not at full strength. They were without injured regulars Joe Francis and Harry Shepherd, but had the brilliantly spectacular newcomer George Newton, experienced England international Stan Greatrex, the veteran former British Champion Roger Frogley, and they had drafted in two fairly inexperienced newcomers in Mike Erskine and Fred Leavis. However, the biggest name on the programme was the idol of the Old Kent Road fans, Tom Farndon. He was, at the time, undoubtedly the best speedway rider in the world. At the age of twenty-four he had reached the very top of his profession. His celebrity status is today matched only by pop icons, film stars and footballers.

At one point in his meteoric career he held all the National League (First Division) track records. He was superbly spectacular and magnificently consistent, and was said to possess the perfect combination of skill, judgment and daring. As if he had not been blessed with gifts enough, he was also devastatingly handsome. Tom Farndon typified the unquenchable spirit of adventurous youth. His remarkable ability had seen him achieve fame – and fortune – comparable only with that of the pioneer Australians who had brought the sport to Britain a mere seven years earlier. Tom Farndon's good looks and pleasant personality resulted in a huge fan following, particularly among young women, and his sheer talent for speedway racing earned him not only the admiration of his peers but the solid achievement of winning every contemporary dirt-track championship there was to be won.

The night's visiting captain, Jack Parker, who had once been a team-mate at Coventry when Tom was just starting out, tended not to be dazzled by the Farndon hyperbole. Years later he was to damn his brilliant rival with faint praise; 'Of course,' said Parker, 'Tom Farndon was *just* a speedway rider.' What he meant was: as opposed to being an all-round motorcyclist like himself. But at the time, the Farndon achievements challenged Parker's status as England's best. Jack was the supreme egotist and Tom had won the London Riders' Championship two years in succession. He had held the British Championship for more than a year, and although Parker was holder of the prestigious Star Championship title, Tom had won it in 1933 and was favourite to knock Parker off his perch in the 1935 Final at Wembley the very next night, 29 August.

The 1935 speedway season had hardly begun when Tom set up a new track record at New Cross, and in so doing he became the first speedway rider in the sport's history to complete four laps of a track from a standing start in under one minute. In June he fended off the challenge of Hackney's Dick Case for the British title he had taken from Wimbledon's Vic Huxley the year before. By then he had worn the crown longer than any other rider. Such was the standing of the competition at the time that New Cross supporters chartered twenty-two motor coaches to travel to cheer on Tom in his deciding match against Case at Wembley. His form was indeed remarkable. Both the British and the Star championships involved the elite of world speedway who treated the paying public to the finest and most spectacular exhibitions of individual racing.

To say that Tom Farndon, and New Cross, were on a high on Wednesday 28 August 1935, would not be an exaggeration. The eager enthusiasts who crammed into the stadium rightly anticipated a hugely exciting meeting with its highly-charged local derby atmosphere. There were plenty of fans from both sides – the blue and gold team colours of the visitors contrasting sharply with the orange and black of the home supporters.

It was a star-studded meeting. As well as the top names appearing in the match, there was the added bonus of West Ham's Bluey Wilkinson riding in the second-half scratch races. London promotions were in the habit of booking in big names to spice up their second halves. Not only were the top riders readily available, but New Cross could hold up to 30,000 people. Mockford and Smith were easily able to afford an extra star attraction, and Bluey might even bring over some of his Custom House fans to pull through the turnstiles yet more paying customers.

It wasn't New Cross's night. They lost to Parker's Harringay 30–41. Tom scored only 8 points when maybe a 12-point maximum could have been expected. It didn't go right for him from the start; he suffered an engine failure in his first ride, Heat 2, leaving Norman Parker and Les Wotton to take a 5–1 lead for Harringay with Roger Frogley third.

In his second ride in Heat 4, Jack Parker got the better of him with Frogley again third. But with Bill Pitcher last at least New Cross shared the points. Tom won his third ride in Heat 9, leading Jack Ormston and Phil Bishop past the chequered flag. In this race Frogley was replaced by Fred Leavis who failed to score, so it was another shared heat.

Finally, in Heat 11, Tom won again, from Norman Parker and Phil Bishop. Fred Leavis, who had this time replaced Mike Erskine, was again last. It was yet another shared heat.

In a special match race after the interval, Bluey Wilkinson beat Ron Johnson. Then, in the New Cross Scratch Race series, Ron Johnson and Stan Greatrex knocked out the Harringay pair Jack Parker and Phil Bishop in Heat 1. In Heat 2, Tom finished ahead of Bluey Wilkinson with Norman Parker third and Bill Pitcher failing to finish. So the night's main final was between Johnson, Greatrex, Farndon and Wilkinson, who all lined up on the starting grid. One spectator gave this eyewitness account of what happened. He said:

From the tapes Ron took a slight lead with Tom second, but with fewer than two yards separating his back wheel from Tom's front. More than

Tom's team-mate Stan Greatrex was involved in the fateful race that cost Tom his life.

a little halfway down the back straight on the third lap, the New Cross skipper touched the fence and fell. So close was Tom that there was never the slightest possibility of his avoiding the crash or laying down his machine. Tom and his machine were thrown into the air, and he was flung an incredible distance before falling on his head. It looked from the terraces as if Tom deliberately turned, to try and hit the fallen machine instead of the man. You have to remember that Ron and Tom had virtually carried the team for several months; they were, in less than a minute, put out of action at a single blow.

Both riders were removed from the track and taken to the Miller General Hospital, Greenwich. Tom's wife Audrey was in the crowd and had seen the crash. Bluey Wilkinson, the fourth rider in that fateful race, had seen it all right in front of him. He said later that he had sensed 'something was going to happen' and had deliberately stayed out of the way. Bluey, of course, was also in the following night's Star Final, and may well have decided on a prudent approach to what was, after all, an unimportant race compared with the big night to come.

The race was re-run and *Speedway News* magazine, the leading speedway journal of the day, in its account of the meeting, reported that 'Wilkinson finished alone . . . his time: 63.8 and Greatrex had pulled out after being filled up.'

Ron Johnson escaped serious injury – no broken bones, but he was badly bruised and had severe lacerations to an arm. It was enough to keep him out of the next night's Star Final at Wembley. However, Tom's injuries were far more serious. Such was his following that regular bulletins on Tom's condition were posted on the hospital gates. Passing tram and omnibus drivers stopped their vehicles outside so that their passengers could read the notices.

Two days after the crash, Tom died without regaining consciousness. By ten o'clock that evening the crowds – including hundreds of weeping women – had grown so big at the hospital gates that police had to be called to control the multitude. Many of Tom's female fans had collapsed when his death was posted and had to receive medical attention. Several vowed they would never visit a speedway track again. One said, 'Everyone loved Tom Farndon. He was such a wonderful rider and one of the cleanest and most unspoilt stars of the tracks.'

The accident was recorded by *Speedway News* – in small type – on page twelve. The headline read, 'A black night for New Cross', and the report said, 'Last Wednesday night was the culmination of the blackest period in the history of New Cross speedway or, for that matter, of London Motor Sports Ltd. Tom Farndon fought for life for forty-eight hours.'

Speedway News reported Tom as saying, ironically, 'If I ever have a serious crash I shall retire.' He was, said the feature, 'perhaps the most colourful rider of his day. The harder the race the better Farndon liked it, nor was he wont to make an excuse on the rare occasions when he had to acknowledge defeat. The limitless adulation he received when a mere youngster would have turned most heads, but Farndon remained modest and unassuming to the last. No champion of any sport has ever worn his laurels so gracefully.'

Champion Of Speedway Badly Hurt

TOM FARNDON, British speedway champion, is on the danger list at the Miller General Hospital, Greenwich, as a result of a crash on the New Cross Speedway last night.

It occurred during the last event of the match.

Ron Johnson, the New Cross captain, was travelling very fast when he struck the safety fence and was flung several yards along the track.

Farndon, his team mate, was following and had no chance to avoid a collision.

Tom Farndon

He struck Johnson's fallen machine, shot in the air, somersaulted and landed on his head.

Both men were taken to hospital, where it was found that Farndon was suffering from serious concussion.

Johnson was treated for shock and had a severe laceration on one of his arms, but was not detained.

The " Daily Herald " was told late last night at the hospital that the champion's condition was grave. Mrs. Farndon was at his bedside.

The *Daily Herald* report of Tom's crash, 29 August 1935.

2

CARRY ON CRASHING . . .

(Coventry, 1928–9)

'There is no limit to his possibilities when he can temper his natural dash and courage with the riper judgment that will soon be his.'

Tom was born on 11 September 1910 at 16 Henrietta Street in the Foleshill district of Coventry, the son of Thomas and Emily Farndon, both Coventry born and bred. The twenty-two-year-old Thomas Senior had married Emily Style, two years his junior, in 1907. One year later, in 1908, their first child, Hilda, was born, followed two years later by Tom. After Tom, there was to be one more addition to the Farndon family, brother Sid, who also went on to be a speedway rider.

Thomas senior was a general haulier by profession and young Tom would often help out on his rounds because school held no particular attraction for him. He left when he was fourteen. At the age of twelve he was already taking the large carthorses from Foleshill to Birmingham for his father. In fact, Tom grew to love the carthorses so much that he fancied being a jockey and one racehorse owner took him on for a month to see how he liked it. But, fortunately for speedway, he didn't care for racehorses as much as did for the carthorses and gave up the idea.

Tom's father liked a drink and would contrive to stop off at every pub they came across on their way home. As a young lad, Tom just wanted to get home and it may have been this experience that led to him being a lifelong teetotaller. Tom called every pub the Oak because there was an Oak near to their home along the Foleshill Road so, as a youngster, he just assumed that every pub was called so. He used to tell his mother when they got home that Dad had wanted to stop off at every Oak on the way home.

On leaving school, Tom was apprenticed as a body-builder at the Rover Works. In his early teens he developed a great love of speed, and when he

Tom's brother, Sid, in
New Cross colours.

SID FARNDON.
NEW CROSS SPEEDWAY.
PROMOTORS—LONDON MOTOR SPORTS LTD.
F. E. MOCKFORD, MANAGING DIRECTOR.
PHOTO—T. H. EVERITT, UPPER NORWOOD, S.E. 19.

was about sixteen he started experimenting with motorcycles belonging to his friends. He used to pull them to pieces and reconstruct them and never lost an opportunity to sneak off for a joyride. Many years later, when Tom's son Roy went for an interview to join the police force, the chief constable told him that the first person he had ever pulled over for speeding was Tom. Unfortunately this recklessness resulted in plenty of spills and his father had to pay for his friends' broken bikes. So, in the end, Farndon senior bought him a bike of his own, a 1914 fixed gear Triumph, but it wasn't a great success as it kept breaking down and they finished up having to push it everywhere. Tom soon scrapped this bike and bought a two-stroke Radco, which caught fire on four occasions. The final outbreak occurred in front of a big firm of silk manufacturers, whose staff quenched the flames with their fire extinguishers. The firm then asked Tom to replace the extinguishers, but, as he couldn't, he gave them his bike instead. He then had to save up for a new bike which took him several months, but eventually he was able to buy a New Imperial.

However, life for the teenager wasn't all about speed and motorcycles. Tom was also a very keen dancer, but he was so shy that he would never ask any of the girls to trip the light fantastic. Hilda's husband Joe used to say to him, 'Tell me which one you want,' and he would make the introductions. It was thanks to one of these introductions that, at the age of sixteen, he first met, and fell in love with, his future wife Audrey, who was an usherette at the local Regal Cinema. This was in spite of the fact that he was wearing short trousers. But there was a reason for this and that was so that he could get into the cinema as a child and pay half price. He continued to do this even after he started going out with Audrey. It didn't seem to put her off him; she just used to think he was tight-fisted. Audrey later left the Regal to become a milkmaid. She would do her rounds on a bicycle with a milk churn on the side.

Tom's love of speed, and in particular motorcycles, was a common feature for the young men in the Coventry area. There were a number of motorcycle clubs around and it was the centre of much competitive activity. In particular the Coventry Motor Cycle Football Club (CMCFC) was one of the leading clubs in the country and actually staged the first international match ever seen in the UK when they took on an Austrian touring side on 16 June 1928 at Highfield Road. The crowd for this match was in the region of 10,000. One of CMCFC's leading riders was Syd Jackson, a rider who was to go on to become one of the country's top speedway riders. Grasstrack racing was also popular in the area and a new track was opened on Coventry Road, Hinckley, in 1928.

It wasn't just on the track that motorcycles seemed to be making their mark in Coventry. In July 1928 Inspector Dreghorn of the local constabulary said that the practice of driving motorcycles at an excessive speed had become such a great nuisance in the city that it was hoped the courts would make an example of some of the offenders by suspending their licences. Alderman W.R. Goate agreed with him adding that, 'Magistrates are determined to put a stop to this dangerous driving.' In two cases, which came before the courts in July 1928, one man was fined £5 and had his licence suspended for three months while the other was fined £1 and suspended for one month.

While all this excitement was going on in the motorcycle world, an entirely new and different sport came to the city of Coventry. On 7 April 1928, a new greyhound track was opened at Lythalls Lane, Foleshill. Several thousand people attended the opening meeting at the well appointed stadium. The entrance to the track was an attractively designed structure while the enclosure inside was bigger even than the one at Coventry City's football ground and equipped with a number of grandstands.

Given Coventry's love of motorcycles, it was inevitable that before long this brand new stadium would fall victim to that other craze that was sweeping the country in 1928 – dirt-track racing. The first official meeting in Great Britain was held at High Beech on 19 February 1928. Such was the attraction that this new sport held for people, by the summer dozens of new tracks had opened, from Brighton in the south to Glasgow in the north.

In the same week that the two motorcyclists were fined for reckless driving on the roads of Coventry, an announcement was made in the *Coventry Herald* that, 'A motor cycling dirt track is in course of construction at Foleshill,' inside the greyhound stadium. The new cinder track was approximately 352 yards long, meaning that it was five laps to the mile. New spring netting was placed round the outer edge of the track to act as a safety fence, while a new paddock area was constructed for the bikes. The manager of the new track was Mr Jack Marshall.

The new Foleshill track opened on 21 July with a good sized crowd of some 3,000, though it was unfortunate that the meeting clashed with a local derby motorcycle football match between Coventry and Birmingham. The official opening was performed by C.J.P. Dodson, the winner of that year's Isle of Man Senior TT race. The biggest thrills of the afternoon were provided by the Australian Irvine Jones and the New Zealander Spencer Smokey Stratton who, along with Dalton of Manchester, demonstrated the art of broadsiding to the captivated crowd. The winner of the open Challenge Final was Gus Kuhn, later to make his name as captain of the Stamford Bridge team, winners of the first Southern League competition the following year.

With the new track being so close to the young, motorcycle-mad Tom Farndon's Foleshill home, it is highly likely that he would have gone along to the opening, but whether to take part in this meeting or as a spectator is unfortunately not known, if indeed he went at all, and is really a matter for speculation. What is known is that the seventeen-year-old Tom did take to the track on 18 August and won his heat of the International Dirt-track Trophy, riding his stripped-down road bike, the New Imperial, in a time of 2 minutes 25.4 seconds for five laps, just under 25 seconds slower than the track record held by Clem Beckett at 2 minutes 0.6 seconds. This was as far as he got. In the semi-final he suffered 'a series of spills.'

THE COVENTRY HERALD.

DIRT TRACK RACING : NEW MOTOR CYCLE SPORT INTRODUCED LOCALLY.

A good-sized crowd assembled at the Greyhound Racing Track, Foleshill, on Saturday afternoon last, to witness the introduction to Coventry of the new motor cycle sport—dirt-track racing. The official opening of the dirt track was performed by C. J. P. Dodson, winner of this year's Senior T.T. Race (as illustrated in the lower picture). The photograph at the side shows a competitor who came to grief during one of the races.

The opening of Foleshill Speedway as reported in the *Coventry Herald*.

Tom was back again the following week, this time competing in the Junior Challenge Race. The *Coventry Chronicle* reported that in heat 2, 'A.E. Willson and Farndon were soon left to fight out the heat between them but Farndon crashed into the netting at the south end of the track, and Willson won by ¾ of a lap in 2 minutes 16.8 seconds.'

In spite of his tendency to find himself in a series of spectacular falls, the young Farndon made his first final on 15 September in the Senior Challenge Race. With riders of the calibre of Syd Jackson, Arthur Jervis and Wilmot Evans in the race, Tom finished nowhere, but already, with only about a month's experience behind him, he was able to mix it with some big names of those early days and was not being overawed by them.

The Foleshill track soon proved to be not enough for the motorcycle enthusiasts of Coventry and on 6 October another speedway venue opened in the city, this time at Brandon. This new track was 'D' shaped and was also 352 yards in length.

The opening meeting was dominated by the BSA works rider from Birmingham, Jack Parker, a man already staking his claim to be England's best speedway rider and indeed the equal of many of the Australians. To prove this was the case, Parker defeated the prominent Australian, Sig Schlamm, in a special match race that night.

Brandon ran only a couple of meetings that season and as Foleshill also closed on 13 October, Tom Farndon was left kicking his heels over the winter waiting for the new season to start. As it happened, Foleshill did not reopen for speedway in 1929 but Brandon was open early in the year for a series of practice sessions. Tom, still mounted on his stripped-down New Imperial, went along to this new track to take part but he kept on crashing. In fact, he never seemed to get round more than two laps without a crash. Although he couldn't finish a race he was nevertheless doing enough to show some potential if only he had a decent bike. One afternoon, a director of the track noticing this lent him a proper speedway bike, a Dirt-track Douglas. On his very first ride on his new mount he managed to complete all four laps, but even more astonishingly he was only two-fifths of a second off the track record. This remarkable ride brought him to the attention of local motorcycle dealer, and another Brandon director, Stanley Glanfield. Glanfield had been one of those influential in bringing speedway to the UK, as it was partly his eye-witness accounts of racing in Australia and his support for A.J. Hunting's International Speedways that helped launch dirt-track racing in Britain.

Glanfield did a deal with Tom that he would supply a machine free of charge in return for a share of any money Tom won. However, when Tom's brother-in-law, Joe, saw how much Glanfield was creaming off he said, 'Forget that!' and bought Tom a speedway bike of his own. Although he now had a

OPENING OF THE BRANDON SPEEDWAY.

" Coventry Herald " Photo.

The new Speedway which was opened at Brandon last Saturday afternoon, in the presence of three thousand spectators, has an excellent track. Giving five laps to the mile, it is commodious and fast. That it is as safe as a dirt track can possibly be was clearly demonstrated by the complete absence of anything serious enough to describe as an accident. Even minor spills were very few. The riders were loud in their praise of the track, and the spectators had good reason to be satisfied with the fare provided, for it was indeed first-rate. The track was opened in the same way that a new road is usually made available for public use. A tape was stretched across by the judges' box. All the riders lined up behind it, and at the appointed time Mrs. S. T. Glanfield, wife of the Managing Director of Motordromes, Ltd., cut the tape with a pair of scissors. The riders then traversed the track several times before the programme proper was proceeded with.

The opening of Brandon Speedway as reported in the *Coventry Herald.*

brand new bike, a Douglas, Tom still seemed to have a penchant for falling and the first time out on his new bike he crashed again. It was soon realised that one of the problems the young Farndon was coming up against was that he had very short arms and the handlebars were not suitable for him. Once these were adjusted, Tom found his new mount much better than his stripped-down road bike.

League speedway in Britain began in 1929 and Coventry entered the new Southern League. On 2 May they had the honour of racing in the first league meeting, losing 31–11 to West Ham on the Londoners' track at Custom House.

The Coventry team for that first match was Lew Lancaster, Alan Saunders, Willmot Evans, W. Tandy, Cyril Lord, Arthur Shene and J. Cloke. Evans was the only Coventry rider to win a race, beating Harold Tiger Stevenson and Jack Adams. Although still attached to Coventry, Jack Parker was not allowed to race for the team because he was a 'Star' rider. Soon after the pioneer promoters, A.J. Hunting and John S. Hoskins, had brought the Australian invaders to England there grew up a Star system as a measure of a rider's ability. It was to distinguish the top talent from the also-rans. To avoid bruising any egos, there was to be no No.1; Jack Parker was No.3. These Star riders were excluded from the league and had to continue appearing in individual trophy events and match races only.

Once the practising was over and the season proper started at Brandon on 4 May, Tom rode in second-half events. Such was his improvement that he finally made the team on 1 June, in Coventry's fourth league match, a home fixture against Wembley. In front of a crowd of 6,600, Tom rode with Lew Lancaster in the first heat, coming in third behind his partner and Wembley's Len Reeve to score his first league point and help secure his team a 27–14 victory.

A fortnight later, Tom took part in the Brandon Open Handicap and found himself up against another young newcomer, Jack Parker's brother, Norman. Norman had started out as Jack's mechanic but then decided to have a go himself. Both Tom and Norman won their preliminary heats to find themselves in the Handicap proper. Tom was drawn

West Ham's Tiger Stevenson.

in Heat 2 against his more experienced team partner, Lew Lancaster. In spite of his greater experience, Lancaster could not shake off Tom as the two tore round the track in a neck-and-neck struggle. It was only when Tom's chain came off on the final bend that Lancaster was able to pull away. Tom started to push for the finishing line as the first two went through to the next round, but as he did so his chain suddenly gripped on the sprocket again and, as the engine was still running, the machine made a dive forward and spun round onto the grass, dragging Tom after it, putting him out of the race altogether.

Tom's first recorded victory in a league match came on 13 July when he won Heat 5 of the match against White City. Tom also went on to win that evening's scratch race final. Even better news was to come when, two weeks later, somewhat ironically as events were later to turn out, he scored his first maximum, winning all three of his races in Coventry's 46–17 annihilation of Crystal Palace.

Tom was also riding in open meetings at Wolverhampton at this time. On 23 July, for example, he competed in their Golden Gauntlet event. In the five-man final, Tom finished second to Geoff Siddaway, just beating Dusty Jenkins after a hectic race. The local newspaper made a special note that Tom's cornering was 'really brilliant work.' A week later he won the Golden Sash final from Ivan Anslow, Tommy Deadman, George Milton and George Allbrook. Again it was a very exciting race with Tom providing most of the excitement.

Already, the eighteen-year-old, with just a year's experience on the dirt tracks, was beginning to be a rider to fear and fast becoming Coventry's top man. When he could stay on the bike he would almost invariably win his team races, but Tom, because he was still perfecting the style that would soon make him one of the most spectacular riders ever to grace the speedway track, was still finding some difficulty in actually finishing a race. There were a number of occasions when he either did not manage to complete a heat, falling in the most dramatic way, or lost yards through almost colliding with the safety fence. For example in the match against Perry Barr on 3 August, he easily won his first race, but then in the second, while holding a 5–1 with his partner, Wilmot Evans, he crashed on the last bend, and then in his third and final race he nearly fell early on finding himself in last place. However, such was his speed that he managed to pass Joe Dallison on the last bend to take a thrilling second place.

Two weeks later he took part in an individual meeting at Brandon. The local newspaper reported, 'A feature of the programme was the clever riding of Tom Farndon, who returned 76.4 in a scratch race.' Because this was an individual event, Coventry star Jack Parker also took part. His best time of the evening was only slightly better than Tom's at 75.2. Once again however, it was a fall that let Tom down. Riding in the final of the evening's Handicap Event, after easily winning his semi-final, he fell, badly injuring his leg.

The blue and gold sash Tom won at Wolverhampton in 1929.

In an article in the Coventry programme at about this time, the writer said of Tom that, 'even in his present state he has accomplished great feats, and there is no limit to his possibilities when he can temper his natural dash and courage with the riper judgment that will soon be his.' Very prophetic words.

His leg injury put him out for a week, but he returned on 24 August only to crash again in an individual event. Up against fellow team-members Lew Lancaster, Arthur Tiny Timms and George Allbrook, he established a big lead and was heading for victory when he fell on the last bend. Once again his injury prevented him from riding for a couple of weeks, making his comeback on 14 September for a league match against London White City.

On his return, Tom continued to show his great potential and on 12 October 1929, the *Coventry Herald* reported that:

A crowd of 8,000 were given excellent value for their money by the [Coventry riders'] performances, chief among which was that of Tom Farndon, who followed up his capital exhibition of the previous week by again taking everything by storm. Farndon provided all that was best in the way of thrills during the evening in his special match race with Tommy Croombs (Lea Bridge) providing a struggle of real first-class order. In defeating his opponent in two straight runs, Farndon recorded the excellent times of 78.2 and 78.4, but his achievement cannot be judged on the actual speed, for there was a great deal more in it than that. In defeating Croombs, Farndon undoubtedly excelled himself, and gave his finest show yet. The first round was a most exciting affair. Getting away together splendidly, both men were abreast at the first bend, but Farndon, who was inside, managed to scrape a yard or two ahead and came down the straight at great pace just a little ahead.

Brandon 1929. From left to right: Max Grosskreutz, Tom, Wilmot Evans.

This he managed to maintain by splendid riding until practically the same position obtained in the second lap. Then Croombs made a superb effort to get in front, and succeeded, but a lap later he lost his lead again, a fine spurt bringing Farndon ahead to win the inside position on the last bend, and victory. Round two was even more thrilling. This time, Croombs established a very useful lead, when, starting inside, he took the first bend in a very clever manner. Going 'all-out', Farndon gradually closed in the gap as the laps went by, but when the last lap commenced it looked fairly easy for Croombs to record a victory. The Lea Bridge rider, however, made the mistake of riding a trifle too wide when approaching the last bend, and before he had time to make good, Farndon, by a brilliant piece of opportunism, had flashed by to win with a yard or so to spare and contribute a rare finish indeed. But Farndon did not stop there, for he was also the successful rider in the final of the Golden Helmet competition, this win entitling him to keep the trophy until next season.

The magnitude of the youngster's victory and how far he had come in such a short time can be shown by the fact that the following week, Croombs defeated Coventry star Jack Parker in a match race series.

The season therefore ended on a very high note for Tom. He had progressed a long way from the novice who kept falling off to become a rider who could take on and beat some of the best riders in the country. As if this wasn't enough, Tom, with his fair curly hair and passive blue eyes with their hint of quiet strength and steadfastness, was a very handsome young man and was beginning to set hearts a-flutter among the young female supporters, though he was only interested in Audrey and they continued to go out together, especially – over the winter months – to the dance halls in and around Coventry. They won both a tango and a Charleston competition at the Coventry Hippodrome – the prize for winning the Charleston competition was a clock.

3

RISING STAR

(Coventry, 1930)

His spectacular style brought the crowds flocking in to see this new sensation at whichever track he was appearing.

Towards the end of the 1929 season, Tom had been promoted to star status. However, with league speedway proving its popularity, star riders were allowed into the teams for the 1930 season, so the Coventry line-up read: Jack Parker, Norman Parker, George Allbrook, John Deeley, Lew Lancaster, Tiny Timms, Bill Stanley, Australian Cecil Walker and, of course, Tom Farndon.

Coventry opened the season on Easter Monday with home and away league fixtures against local rivals Leicester. The home meeting at Brandon went off smoothly. Tom was out in the second heat against the Leicester star, Squib Burton. For three laps the pair of them rode neck-and-neck until Burton fell, leaving Tom to coast to an easy victory. Tom contributed two wins that night to his team's comprehensive 34–19 rout of their opponents.

So far so good, but it was the away fixture at Leicester that was to cause ructions throughout the speedway world. Leicester were seeking revenge for their afternoon drubbing, but they were up against a very confident outfit. The match itself proved to be a very exciting affair and with one heat to go the scores were level, everything resting on the last heat. Leicester's pair for that notorious race were former Coventry motorcycle football star Syd Jackson and Billy Ellmore, while Tom and Tiny Timms were out for Coventry. As they went into the first bend, Jackson, Tom and Timms were in a line with Jackson sandwiched between the two Coventry riders. Whether intentionally or not, Tom and Timms frustrated Jackson by drawing together. To avoid a crash, Jackson attempted to pull up but in so doing touched Timms who wobbled violently and went across the path of Ellmore who was just behind, causing both of them to fall. With Jackson also down,

Tom with his 1930 Coventry captain, Jack Parker. This photograph was actually taken two years later at Wembley when both men had become an integral part of the England Test team.

only Tom was left still sitting in the saddle and the red lights were put on to stop the race.

Jackson immediately lodged a complaint that Farndon had 'chopped' him. There was a fifteen-minute delay while the ACU steward considered what to do. During this interval, the large contingent of Coventry supporters gave vent to their feelings while the Leicester supporters became equally vociferous. At one point the whole situation got out of hand and several blows were exchanged. Jackson, the Leicester hero, rode round trying to pacify the crowd but even he was unable to prevent the many fights that had now broken out. Eventually, the ACU steward, Mr Topping, announced that the race would be re-run with the exclusion of Farndon. The Coventry riders did not accept this verdict and Timms refused to race in the re-run, supported by his manager, Stan Glanfield. Consequently, Leicester were awarded 5 points to take the match 29–24.

The Leicester management believed that it was the right decision as Jackson had been badly sandwiched; the Coventry management were equally adamant that the crash had been caused by Jackson throttling back and that Tom was completely blameless. As if all this wasn't enough, a new fact came to light after the meeting had finished which was that Mr Topping said he didn't put on the red lights to stop the race and didn't know who had.

Following this incident, Coventry complained to the Southern League management committee. As well as demanding the match be awarded to them rather than Leicester, they also wanted to know who decided to stop the race by putting on the red lights and why the steward took so long to make his decision. The following week, the Leicester manager, Norman Coates, wrote a long letter to the *Speedway News* in which he said that it was the Clerk of the Course who put on the red lights under ACU Regulation 40 which stated that the Clerk of the Course could stop the race at any time if, in his opinion, it was dangerous to let it continue, and that the ACU steward had taken a long time because he was very thorough. He had interviewed all the officials and riders involved in the incident before coming to his decision. On the substantive matter of Tom's exclusion, Coates said that, without suggesting Farndon was guilty of intentional dangerous riding, during the day's events, five of the Leicester riders had fallen while racing against Farndon. Having raised the spectre of Tom's questionable tactics, as he saw it, he then added, 'However, that is beside the point.'

The Southern Speedway League Management Committee subsequently upheld the steward's decision causing Glanfield to lodge a formal appeal with the ACU. Eventually the ACU upheld the decision. The whole incident was unprecedented in the history of the sport at that time and although appeals, counter-appeals, refusals to ride and, fortunately less so, opposition supporters coming to blows are not exactly everyday occurrences now, they are not unheard of. But this was the first time any or all of these incidents had happened in an official speedway fixture in Britain. And it was Tom Farndon who was at the centre of the controversy.

It might be thought that all this would have an adverse effect on the nineteen-year-old youngster as he tried to make his way in the sport, but he was able to shrug it all off as though nothing had happened. In the following week's meeting, against Belle Vue, he beat Australian star Max Grosskreutz by a distance in Heat 2, while the week after he scored a maximum against West Ham, giving a breathtaking display of broadsiding around the Brandon circuit.

By the middle of May, the strength of the Coventry outfit was beginning to show as they topped the league table. However, the team suffered a severe blow towards the end of the month when the lorry on which their bikes were being transported to London for a match against Lea Bridge caught fire near Fenny Stratford and all their bikes were badly damaged or destroyed. Glanfield and Australian ace Frank Arthur managed to scrape together some bikes for the team to enable the match to go ahead.

Once again, Tom, showing his coolness under pressure and his keen racing brain, managed to win Heat 1 even on a borrowed bike he had never seen before. He then crashed in his second ride and Coventry fell behind, losing the fixture, 31–22.

However, the good form of the Coventry team continued with Tom now firmly in place as the team's number two to Jack Parker. This two-pronged spearhead was a match for any other top two in the league and Coventry retained their top place until the end of June, at which time *Speedway News* published all the riders' averages. Tom was now no longer second to Jack Parker in the Coventry outfit. He had overtaken him to sit on top with a calculated match average (cma) of 8.64 to Parker's 7.56. In the overall league averages, Tom was in seventh place, behind the likes of Jack Ormston and Frank Arthur but above some of the sport's established stars such as Vic Huxley, Wal Phillips, Tiger Stevenson and Ron Johnson. At just nineteen years old, there was no doubt that Tom was fast emerging as one of the stars of the sport, and not just that. His spectacular style brought the crowds flocking in to see this new sensation at whichever track he was appearing, and he was beginning to pick up invitations to appear in individual events and second halves around the country. For example, on 20 May, he again rode at Wolverhampton in a three-leg match race against team-mate Norman Parker. Tom won Heat 1 although engine failure allowed Parker to win Heat 2. The third heat was a thrilling affair which Tom narrowly lost. There was good compensation in the second half when he won the Wolverhampton Scratch Race final. Then, on 10 June in a Star match race, he appeared at Tredegar where he beat Billy Lamont in two straight runs, lowering Sprouts Elder's track record by one second in the process.

BRITISH CHAMPIONSHIP.

RON JOHNSON. (HOLDER.)
VERSUS
SYD JACKSON. (CHALLENGER.)

Syd Jackson, left, shakes hands with Ron Johnson before the British Individual Championship in 1933. Both riders played a major role in Tom's career at different times. Jackson was involved in a number of controversies with Tom in his early days while Johnson was Tom's captain at Crystal Palace and New Cross.

As if the previous controversy surrounding Tom wasn't enough, he found himself at the centre of another big hullabaloo, again involving Syd Jackson, when he was excluded during an open meeting at Brandon for jumping the start. Because Nottingham had given notice that they would be unable to fulfil their league fixture, the Coventry management organised an evening of individual scratch races, handicap races and match races. For the Golden Gauntlet scratch race championship a new method of starting was tried out in an effort to ensure a fair start by all four riders. All races at that time were started under the rolling start rules, but riders often managed to gain an unfair advantage coming up to the line. The experiment called for a pacer, Al Wilkinson, to ride the initial lap on a road machine with the other riders having to keep level with him so that as the race started they would all be together. If the steward was satisfied that the riders were together, the green light would go on and the four riders would continue with the pacer dropping out. Each competing rider was warned that should there be three false starts in any heat, whoever jumped the start a fourth time would be disqualified. In the first semi-final of the Golden Gauntlet, Tom was up against Syd Jackson. As

Coventry v. Wimbledon, 15 May 1930. Tom is no. 3.

the green light went on Tom was seen to get a good lead which he maintained until the end of the race, but the steward, Mr Winckle, then announced that he had been excluded for jumping the start and the race was awarded to Jackson. There was uproar in the stadium as soon as the announcement was made, and Tom came out from the pits to speak to the officials as the noise around the stadium increased. It was some time before the programme could continue. The exclusion was upheld and Tom was out. Jackson went on to win the Golden Gauntlet final. To make up for the crowd's disappointment an extra race was added to the evening and Tom took on Jackson in a special match race. In a magnificent display of broadsiding, Tom won easily.

The controversy over Tom's exclusion continued for several weeks, his supporters claiming it was very unfair for Tom to have been excluded for breaking a rule which was being experimented with for the first time. They also felt that if Tom was to be excluded, the green light should not have come on, the race should have been stopped right away and he ought not to have been allowed to race on thinking he was fighting for a place in the final.

Mr Herbert Cooper, chairman of the Coventry Supporters' Club, wrote to the ACU to complain about the steward's decision. He was concerned that the decision was such a bad one that it might put people off coming to speedway again. Part of his letter read, 'The announcement revealed a degree of dissatisfaction such as has never been witnessed at Brandon, the effect of which from a gate point of view, cannot yet be estimated.' He went on to call for a full ACU inquiry as he felt the steward's decision was detrimental to the sport. He finished his letter by saying, 'I hold no brief for Farndon; although he is a good and clean rider. Nor do I hold any ill-feeling towards Mr Winckle, but I must add that Farndon is a much better rider than Mr Winckle is a steward.'

On the other side, the local paper printed a letter from someone calling himself Brandon Fan deploring the fact that a great many of his fellow supporters had expressed a 'chorus of disapproval' aimed at the ACU steward. The letter went on to say, 'The continuous false starts are spoiling the game and the patience of the public is becoming exhausted. It is wearying and irritating, and surely on the first attempt of the stewards to make a real effort to stop this abuse that the supporters of the speedway should give vent to boos and hostile demonstrations against the stewards for doing their duty is hardly fair.' Once again, the young Tom took it all in his stride and was back in action as strong as ever for the next meeting.

Tom's position as Coventry's number one was recognised at the end of July when he was appointed temporary captain after Parker had been forced to pull out of a number of meetings owing to an ankle injury. His first match in charge was a baptism of fire with Coventry up against the league champions, Stamford Bridge. But Tom rose magnificently to the occasion and was the hero of a tense encounter which resulted in a single-point victory for his team. Tom won all his races, including one against the reigning Overseas Star Riders' Champion, Frank Arthur, in a time just one-fifth of a second outside Parker's Brandon track record.

In spite of this victory, Parker's absence began to take its toll on Coventry and their winning run faltered. By August they had dropped down the table to fifth place. In September the qualifiers for the Star Championship finals were announced based on the league averages. Tom qualified in eighth place, while Parker did not qualify at all. On the night of the finals he suffered engine failure in his first round match and was knocked out. However, he had done enough to not only establish himself firmly as Coventry's number one rider, but be recognised as one of the best riders in Britain. Not bad for a nineteen-year-old with just one-and-a -half years' experience behind him.

Towards the end of the season the ACU had cause to investigate the management of Coventry speedway and just before the final league match was

Tom, front left, captains Coventry for the first time against Stamford Bridge, July 1930. The Stamford Bridge captain, Frank Arthur is the rider front right.

due to be held, they closed Brandon down 'due to irregularities in connection with the payment of monies due to riders employed by Motordrome Ltd [the owners of Brandon Speedway].' The Managing Director and Company Secretary were suspended.

With uncertainty now hanging over the future of Coventry speedway, Tom felt it wise to look for another club. He went to see a number of possible tracks and met their promoters. Eventually he finished up having tea with the Crystal Palace promoters, Freddie Mockford and Cecil Smith. By the time Mockford called for the bill, Tom was already on the Crystal Palace books. He received nothing by way of a signing-on fee and explained his on-the-spot decision by jokingly suggesting that perhaps Mockford or Smith had put something in his tea. However, it was probably more to do with the fact that Mockford and Smith were both very shrewd operators and could see the potential in the young lad from Coventry. They were not willing to take no for an answer and Tom could see their determination reflected his own and that his best chance of improvement lay with them.

4

VICTIM AND VICTOR

(Crystal Palace, 1931)

It wasn't just Tom's natural talent, it was also his spectacular never-say-die attitude that was endearing him to the thousands. He was fast becoming the idol of the fans.

At Crystal Palace, Tom joined a team full of already established star riders including Ron Johnson, Roger Frogley, Triss Sharp, Clem Mitchell, Joe Francis, Harry Shepherd and George Lovick. Everyone was waiting to see how

Tom with his bike after the back wheel had come off in the match against Lea Bridge on 11 April 1931.

Tom in full-throttle action.

Tom would fit into the team as the Glaziers' league campaign got underway with a match against Lea Bridge. He made a reasonable debut but was plagued by mechanical problems. He was, for example, winning the fifth heat, but coming out of the fourth bend on the last lap his back wheel suddenly parted company with the rest of his bike. Fortunately he was able to pick himself up and stagger over the line with what was left of his motor, gaining second place as the two Lea Bridge riders had previously crashed into each other. In fact, one of them, Howie Osment, finished before Tom but had not commenced his last lap when Shepherd, the winner, crossed the line, so he was disqualified. In spite of this misfortune with his bike, it was a useful debut as he helped his new team to a convincing 31–21 victory.

Tom continued to be beset by bike trouble as he tried to impress his new fans and manager. The next visitors to Crystal Palace were Southampton, and although the Glaziers ran out victors 30–24, Tom once again suffered from multiple engine failures. *Speedway News* reported that the match was 'dismally uninteresting.' Better news followed in the next match when Crystal Palace scored a good victory over Wimbledon, 32–22. Free from engine trouble for once, Tom rode to his first victory in Crystal Palace colours, managing to defeat no less a rider than the Wimbledon and Australia star Dick Case. But it didn't last, and once again Tom found himself the victim of a sick bike in the next encounter with Stamford Bridge. In the one heat he was free of engine problems he rode well, but Palace supporters were beginning to get impatient at his failure to sort his motors out, especially when they could see how well he could go when he was able to.

The following week against Harringay it was the same old story. Tom scored 6 points but in one heat he was leading when his chain broke and he had to wheel home for a single point. Throughout the next couple of months, Tom's form continued to be dictated by the state of his machinery. His expected rise to stardom was halted and he failed to make any real headway. The one match he really wanted to do well in was the one against his former team, Coventry. After their problems at the end of the 1930 season, Coventry were now back in the league, having taken the place of Leicester who had been forced to close down in May. Crystal Palace visited Brandon at the end of June. It was yet another close, thrilling match. Going in to the final heat the score was 26–22 to Coventry, with Crystal Palace needing a 5–1 to level the match. Tom was out for the Glaziers riding alongside his captain, Ron Johnson. With Tom having so far fulfilled his wish to be the best of the visitors by winning his first two races easily, the visiting fans had every hope that they could succeed. To cheers from the away supporters, Tom and his captain immediately went off into the lead, but, as had happened so often before, Tom's machine let him down and he had to pull out. Johnson finished on his own for a 3–3, leaving

Crystal Palace 4 points down, 29–25. Tom had desperately wanted to do well at his old home but it was a very disappointing end for him, knowing that once again his machinery had not only been responsible for losing him the race, but also, in this instance, the match.

Mockford was by now getting very concerned about the state of his young star's equipment and he dropped Tom to reserve for a while to give him a chance to sort himself out. But it wasn't only Tom's bike that was giving cause for concern. By now, Wembley were by far and away the best team in the league, generally overwhelming opponents. Mockford realised that one of the main reasons for this was the care and attention the Wembley management paid to the team's machinery and he was determined to outdo Wembley in this department. With Crystal Palace due to meet Wembley, he made sure that all the team's bikes were stripped down and cleaned, older parts replaced and the engines tuned to perfection. The result was a stunning 30–23 victory over the league leaders and, for the first time that season, it was clear that the Wembley bikes were not as fast as those of their opponents. The Farndon/Francis pairing scored a maximum 15 points, while Johnson scored an individual maximum. Mockford now knew for sure that this was the way to go, so he set up a state-of-the-art workshop at the back of the speedway track in the old polo-pony sheds, fitted with all the best modern appliances for all the team-members to use. Not only that, but he brought in as workshop supervisor the man whose bike frame, along with the JAP engine, had revolutionised the sport; G.L. Wallis. With four assistant mechanics, Mockford made him responsible for ensuring that the Glaziers turned out in every match with the best possible machinery. Johnson, Francis, Key and Shepherd were all given brand new Wallis JAP mounts with another being made for Frogley. After every meeting, Wallis insisted on taking the bikes into the workshop and overhauling them.

The next home match against Southampton underlined the wisdom of Mockford's decision as the Glaziers hammered Southampton 38–15. There was no doubting the fact that their bikes were several miles per hour faster than the Saints' mounts. Johnson recorded the fastest race time ever seen at Crystal Palace when he stormed home in Heat 3 in a time of 79.6 seconds.

For some reason, however, and in spite of his early season form, Tom insisted on continuing to look after his own machine. This wouldn't have been quite so bad if he'd been an expert mechanic, but he wasn't. The Crystal Palace management despaired of Tom as he insisted on fixing his own bike with various coils of copper wire and a large hammer. It was said that Mockford had to employ a special member of staff whose job it was to walk round the track and pick up the bits and pieces that had fallen off Tom's bike during the racing. This is no doubt an apocryphal story but makes the point about Tom's mechanical knowledge.

The next home meeting was the Crystal Palace round of the Star Riders' Championship. A change in the way the qualifiers for the final were to be decided had been announced at the beginning of the season. This year, each club was to hold an elimination contest on its own track to find one of its representatives, while the second would be nominated by the club. It almost goes without saying that Tom's chances of becoming Crystal Palace's representative were ended when he suffered engine failure in the first heat.

Despite his patchy form, Tom had done enough, when his bike allowed him, to show the selectors that he was worth a place in the England team and he was chosen as reserve for the side in the Third Test match against Australia held on 14 August at Wembley. Tom made his debut in Heat 9 coming in as a replacement for Harry Whitfield, managing to score his first point in England colours when he headed home his partner, Colin Watson. He scored another point in Heat 13 thus ending his first Test match with 2 points.

The following week, Tom took part in the London Riders' Championship held at Crystal Palace. He rode well in the preliminary heats to reach the semi-final, where he lost to the eventual winner, Joe Francis, a rider he had beaten in the preliminary round.

The next match, against West Ham, saw Tom win his first two heats and then, inevitably, fail to finish his third because of machine trouble. It was now early September and Mockford was getting totally frustrated with his young would-be star. It was obvious to all that Tom could be a very good, if not a great, rider if only he could get his equipment sorted out. Following a heart-to-heart between promoter and rider, Tom eventually agreed to ride a new Wallis/JAP machine and to use the facilities on offer at the workshops. The results of this change of heart were sensational as Tom finished the season in breathtaking form.

His next outing was at his old stamping ground, Brandon, where he carried all before him, although he was excluded in one race having been judged guilty of boring Coventry rider Bunny Wilcox in one heat, after coming through from third place to take the lead.

Crystal Palace now faced two very important matches. They had reached the final of the London Cup and were up against the all-conquering Wembley in the two-legged final. The first leg was at home and resulted in a magnificent 59–36 win for the Glaziers. Tom, along with team-mates Johnson and Francis, was practically unbeatable. He scored 9 from three races and then fell in his last heat. Johnson scored a maximum 12 points, while Francis also won three heats out of three, having been disqualified in Heat 14 for twice jumping the start.

CRYSTAL PALACE TEAM—LONDON CUP WINNERS, 1931.
Back Row : Jim Cowie, S. Pitcher, Nobby Key, Triss Sharp, Ron Johnson and Tom Farndon.
Front Row :   Alf Sawford, Roger Frogley (Capt.), Harry Shepherd and Joe Francis.

The Crystal Palace team featured on the front cover of *Speedway News* after winning the London Cup in 1931. Back row, left to right: Jim Cowie, Bill 'Skid' Pitcher, Nobby Key, Triss Sharp, Ron Johnson, Tom. Front row: Alf Sawford, Roger Frogley (captain), Harry Shepherd, Joe Francis.

Everything now seemed set for an exciting return leg at Wembley as there was a feeling among supporters of both teams and neutrals that the second leg would consist of a long and keen struggle by the Lions to make up the 23-point deficit, and that the interest would come in seeing if Crystal Palace could hang on enough to take the title.

However, that wasn't how it turned out. It came as something of a shock to the Wembley supporters and as a joyous surprise to the Crystal Palace supporters. Hundreds of them made the trip to the Empire Stadium to cheer on their team and make a colourful orange and black section among the 35,000 crowd, when Tom took charge in the first heat, overwhelming the Wembley captain, Colin Watson, to take it in the very fast time of 79 seconds. So dominant were the Glaziers that by Heat 9 of the sixteen-heat match, the famous Lions needed a 5–0 in every remaining race just to draw. Tom was in a class of his own that night. Not only did he score a maximum, beating the likes of Jack Ormston, Lionel Van Praag, Wally Kilmister and Colin Watson on their own track, but he then went on to win the second-half scratch race trophy, beating Ormston in the final. His win in the Crystal Palace heat was a particularly hair-raising affair as he actually fell during the race with his elbow touching the cinders, but he managed to haul his machine up and continue racing as though nothing had happened.

Just two days after this triumph in the London Cup Final, Crystal Palace performed the unheard of feat of annihilating Manchester (Belle Vue) 45–9, scoring a 5–1 in every single heat. It was the first time a whitewash had been achieved in the history of league speedway and has been repeated only a handful of times since.

There is no doubt that with Tom now seated on reliable equipment, he was showing just what he could do and, although it was too late for the league, there were few who would argue with the fact that Crystal Palace were now the best team in the country. There was a one-off unfortunate return to engine problems for Tom in his next match against Wimbledon when his carburettor came off in Heat 4 and he managed to finish Heat 7 only by holding it on. But he finished the home league season with two more maximums in victories over High Beech, 39–15, and Lea Bridge, 38–15.

However, he wasn't finished yet. In the last away match of the season against Wimbledon, not only did he score a maximum but he also broke the track record, defeating the legendary Wimbledon captain Vic Huxley in the process. In a non-league meeting at Plymouth he lowered their track record and, finally, in a special open meeting at Wembley on 15 October, he equalled the track record.

After a shaky start to the season, mainly owing to his poor equipment, there is no doubt that Tom was now able to match the best riders in the country in ability. He had been chosen to ride for England and had broken two track records and equalled another. But it wasn't just his natural talent, it was also his spectacular never-say-die attitude that was endearing him to the thousands of Crystal Palace supporters. With these two factors in place, he was fast becoming the idol of the fans.

5

DAZZLING DOWN UNDER

(New Zealand, 1931–2)

*'Farndon forged ahead . . . [putting] his machine flat on the cinders, lifting it
erect again as he came out of the corner, still accelerating. In four brilliant laps, Farndon
showed an almost uncanny skill in handling his fast J.A.P. motor.'*

New Zealand Herald

At the end of the 1931 season, Tom, together with his Crystal Palace colleagues, Roger Frogley and Nobby Key, and Wembley's Jack Jackson, travelled to New Zealand to gain more experience. They arrived ready to take part in the meeting at Kilbirnie Stadium, Wellington, on 12 December. Tom's first race came in the second heat of the Big Nine scratch race. He was up against local stars Clarrie Tonks and Harry Mangham. Although Mangham worried away behind him, Tom was never in any real danger of losing his first race on the other side of the world and progressed through to the final. Here he met Frogley and New Zealand's greatest rider of the era, Wally Kilmister. Kilmister was not only the track record holder at Kilbirnie, but was also a prominent member of the peerless Wembley Lions team back in England. As they went into the first bend Tom and Kilmister collided and Tom fell, slightly injuring himself. Although the race was re-run with all four riders eligible to take part, Tom had to withdraw and retired from the rest of the meeting. Apart from winning his first race, it was not exactly the start he was looking for in New Zealand.

From Wellington, Tom moved on to Western Springs in Auckland having his first ride there on 19 December. This time it was a different story and Tom gave an absolutely outstanding display of broadsiding. The *New Zealand Herald*, reporting on his opening race, immediately latched on to the attributes

Tom in New Zealand surrounded by riders, track officials and mechanics.

that had made Tom such a popular performer in England. The newspaper's description of the opening race read:

> From the rolling start, Farndon forged ahead . . . [putting] his machine flat on the cinders, lifting it erect again as he came out of the corner, still accelerating. In four brilliant laps, Farndon showed an almost uncanny skill in handling his fast J.A.P. motor, and remarkable judgment in controlling the short fierce slides that his mount was inclined to develop on account of the great speed. Farndon did

not leave the white line at the inside of the track for five yards and A. Mattson, the Auckland and Dominion champion, who was close behind, could not pass, as he was not fast enough to go round the Englishman, and there was never enough room for him to slip inside. Farndon won the first race in the remarkable time of 1 minute 18.6 seconds, which is by far the fastest time ever made in a match event, being 0.4 second better than the one mile record made by Kilmister, the Wellington champion, at the opening meeting of the season a fortnight earlier . . . He was given a warm reception for his clever work, the cheers being renewed when it was announced that he had beaten the record.

This was the first time Tom had ever seen the track, let alone ridden on it, and yet he had smashed the track record at his first attempt. It was the most brilliant exhibition of speedway riding ever seen at Western Springs.

Following this win and further wins in the first round and semi-final of the Summer Handicap from a 55-yard handicap, Tom again had problems in the final. Here he was up against New Zealand's Alf Mattson again. Once again Tom made the best start but Mattson stayed close behind. On the second lap, Tom hit a bump causing him to swerve from the white line for a second. Mattson saw his chance and immediately lifted his bike bodily, throwing it inside Tom. Just as he did that, Tom recovered his position and the two machines collided. Mattson was just able to control his fall and slid to the ground comparatively gently, but Tom was flung over the handlebars and fell heavily on one shoulder. His rear wheel was badly buckled and the footrest torn off. After receiving treatment from the St John Ambulance officers, Tom took out his reserve bike for the re-run, but he again met with misfortune as he shed a tyre while sliding and only just averted another crash by exercising great skill. His injury, together with the damage to both machines, prevented him from taking part in the rest of the meeting.

Tom's exploits were the talk of Auckland and a record crowd turned up at the next meeting at Western Springs the following week to see the English sensation. They weren't disappointed. In the first event of the night, Tom broke the track record. This was a specially staged attempt on the New Zealand flying start one mile record of 1 minute 16 seconds held by Frank Pearce. After the usual preliminary lap, the yellow flag went down and Tom shot round the first lap in 18.6 seconds. Hugging the inside with uncanny skill he was so close to the grass that frequently a white cloud of dust showed that he was actually riding on the white line. His succeeding laps were 19.2, 19.6 and 19.6 making a total time of 1 minute 17 seconds, which, although one second outside the one mile record, smashed the current track record of 1 minute 18.2 held by Squib Burton.

His first proper race came in the next event, the first heat of the International match between Auckland and England. After some difficulty in securing a fair rolling start, Alf Mattson managed to take an early lead and then rode brilliantly to keep the Englishman out. Time and again Tom tried to find a way through on the inside rounding the corners, but until the last bend Mattson proved unpassable. It was not in Tom's nature ever to give up, and on the last bend he finally out-cornered his opponent and coming down the final stretch managed to increase his lead by five lengths.

In the second heat, Tom won great applause from the crowd by carrying out one of the most daring and skilful feats seen at the stadium, or anywhere else for that matter. In the second lap, his exhaust pipe came adrift, but, with only a slight slackening of speed, he stooped down and secured it. The slight delay however was sufficient to lose him the race and he came in third. He made up for this set back by winning his third heat in the International match by 50 yards.

Tom took part in the next meeting at Western Springs on 31 December, but this time to the great surprise of those present he was passed by Mattson in the second heat of the International event, although he got his revenge later in the evening as he easily defeated the Auckland champion.

From Western Springs, Tom returned to the Kilbirnie track in January. The stadium was packed to see him make another attempt on the one mile record. However, the attempt ended in farce when the flag marshal waved the chequered flag after Tom had completed just three laps. He was offered another go but declined.

In the meeting itself, Tom at last had to give best as he was beaten by Wally Kilmister, but things changed the following week and Tom finally got the measure of his New Zealand opponent. The first time they met was in Heat 1 of a match between the Internationals and Wellington. Although Tom led Kilmister for three-and-a-half laps, he made a slight mistake on the third bend of the last lap, drifting out no more than three yards from the white line, but it was enough to let Kilmister through and he just managed to beat Tom to the line.

After these defeats at the hands of the New Zealand star, Tom was determined that it wouldn't happen again. They next met in the sixth race of a special series of match races. For three full laps the two men hurtled round the track side by side, neither of them giving an inch, but then going into the first bend of the last lap Tom rode magnificently and managed to shake off his opponent to win by a dozen lengths. This was the first occasion on which Kilmister had been beaten from a level start all season. In fact, earlier in the same meeting he had beaten the 1931 Star Champion, Ray Tauser.

After two more successful meetings at Kilbirnie, Tom returned to Western Springs on 30 January where he met the great Australian star, Vic Huxley.

The Kilbirnie Stadium, Wellington.

Tom and Huxley were in the first heat of the International match. Tom got an excellent start and drew ahead round the first bend. Huxley could do nothing and was unable to catch the Englishman. In the second heat, Tom once again showed his mastery over Huxley, winning by a considerable margin. They met for a third time in Heat 3 with the same result, although it has to be said that this time Huxley's motor failed as the two were going in to the first bend on level terms.

They then took part in a special Match Race. This time Tom fell on the first bend but the race was stopped and restarted with both riders. At the second time of asking, Tom gained a lead of about a length going in to the first bend. Huxley worried away behind him and drew level on the third lap, but once again his motor failed and Tom finished alone.

They met once more in the final of the Big Twelve Handicap. This time Huxley was left at the start, while Tom (on 60 yards) took an early lead from J. Gower (on 30 yards). He extended his lead throughout the race and won by half a lap.

The next meeting of Tom and Huxley on 6 February was advertised extensively in the local press:

Champion defends his title! Huxley v Farndon. Two Challenge Match Races! Vic Huxley, champion of the world today, and Tom Farndon, regarded as the coming champion, two of the greatest riders who have ever been seen at Western Springs Speedway, will fight out two special match races . . . Not satisfied with his display last Saturday night, Huxley has challenged Farndon . . . Watch a champion defend his title . . . Watch him endeavour to outwit and out-manoeuvre the brilliant Farndon.

Before the match races, Tom took part in the Big Twelve Handicap and showed he was in top form once again. In the second heat he put up a brilliant performance, establishing a new track record of 1 minute 22.2 seconds from a standing start. Not only did he achieve this from a 60-yard handicap, at one point in the race his machine left the track and broadsided on to the grass but he managed to regain control quickly and carry on.

Tom then followed up his new standing start record by setting a new four-lap rolling start record of 1 minute 17.4 seconds in the first of the challenge match series against Huxley. Tom went ahead at the start and was never in trouble. In the second leg, Huxley had the advantage of the inside berth and took an early lead. Tom made repeated attempts to pass him and both men rode wheel-to-wheel for two laps. Tom once again rode up on the grass but recovered well to take the lead and, in the end, won by a comfortable margin to take the series 2–0.

In Heat 2 of the International match, New Zealand v. Australia v. England, Tom fell leaving Huxley to win the race in fine style. Fortunately, he was not injured and in Heat 3 he managed to beat his main Western Springs rivals Mattson and Huxley easily.

The English team's last meeting in New Zealand at Western Springs on 15 February was a bit of an anti-climax. It should have been a big occasion because Wally Kilmister was booked to appear as well as the usual faces, but in his first race of the evening, he fell heavily, bruising his thigh and he was forced to withdraw from the rest of the meeting. As if this wasn't bad enough, Tom then went out to race Mattson. Mattson took the lead at the first bend while Tom followed close behind making desperate efforts to get inside on the corners. On the last bend of the race his machine touched the grass and sent him spinning out of control. He fell and injured his thumb causing him to withdraw from the meeting as well.

At the end of the meeting, Mr A.C. Jacobs, the chairman of Directors of Auckland Speedways Ltd, came to the microphone to pay tribute to the

Tom arrives in England after his New Zealand success and is welcomed back by his Crystal Palace promoter Fred Mockford and team-mate Nobby Key, left. His travelling companions on the right are Roger and Audrey Frogley.

English riders' sportsmanship. Roger Frogley replied on behalf of the team. In a separate testimonial to Tom personally, Mr Jacobs said, 'I wish to thank you for the consistently good riding you have given at our meetings. The directors also wish to thank you for the manner in which you have always operated with them. I think I can say without contradiction that as far as the Auckland public are concerned you are considered the best rider that has appeared on the track. I am pleased to see that you leave us holding our track record for the mile at 77 seconds, and also for the fastest time in a race at 77.6 seconds. These will take some beating.'

Tom's visit to New Zealand had been an undoubted success. While out there he was interviewed by a local paper, the *New Zealand Free Lance*, which introduced Tom to its readers with the words, 'Tommy Farndon has just turned twenty-one. His face is round and fair – when free of the grime of the dirt-track hits. His hair is curly and powerful. Tommy sees the funny side of everything, and is the merriest of a fearless cinder-shifting bunch.' The interview finished by saying, 'Apart from the dirt track, Farndon is a keen dancer, and his unusual sense of balance has enabled him to win a number of competitions. He has not thrown a leg across a 'pleasure' motor-cycle for a couple of years, but he delights in motoring, and when travelling from speedway to speedway in England covers about a thousand miles a week, usually in his own Rover light six, which he had half-a-mind to bring with him to New Zealand. Asked how the game was panning out financially, Tom smiles with satisfaction: "Not too bad. I have earned as much as £100 a week."'

6

TEST MATCH HERO

(Crystal Palace, 1932)

But his greatest accomplishment of the year was marrying his teenage sweetheart.

Tom, returning to Great Britain with a greatly enhanced reputation, found that the 1932 season had started with the news that he had been selected to take part in a knockout competition to find a challenger for Jack Parker's British Individual Championship (BIC). This was a new competition which had been introduced the previous season to find the best match racer. Vic Huxley was nominated as the first champion with Colin Watson his first challenger. The format of the competition was for the two riders to race against each other in a best-of-three contest at each rider's home track. If this resulted in a draw, a further best-of-three decider would be held on a neutral track. Huxley proved too good for Watson in the first challenge, confirming his position as champion. Following this, riders were then nominated by the Speedway Control Board to take part in a knockout competition to find the next challenger for the title. Jack Parker was successful not only in the competition to find the challenger but also beat Huxley for the title.

In the first challenge round in 1932, Tom was chosen along with Eric Langton, Dick Case, Max Grosskreutz, Arthur Jervis, Frank Arthur, Vic Huxley and Colin Watson. For Tom to be chosen in such illustrious company as a challenger for the title is an indication of the respect he was now accorded by the sport's governing body.

The first round of the British Individual Championship challenges was due to take place in May. Before that, the newly introduced National Speedway Association Trophy got underway. Until the start of this season there had been two leagues, the Northern League and the Southern League. With the Northern League almost in a state of collapse it was agreed to amalgamate the two into one national league. There were to be two league competitions during the year. The first part of the season saw the National Speedway Association Trophy, while the second part saw the inaugural staging of the National League. Crystal Palace's first fixture was away at Plymouth. It was obvious from the start that the Palace team was far superior to that of Plymouth. Heats 1 and 3 resulted in 5–1s for the Glaziers. The only reason Heat 2 did not also result in a 5–1 was because Tom, well ahead at the time, overslid and found himself sitting on the track. Mockford urged him to take things easy as he could practically win as he pleased. Tom earnestly agreed and promised he would not take any more chances. As Heat 4 started he flew away from the other three riders, increasing his lead throughout the race. His time at the end was 78.4 seconds, 0.8 seconds faster than his own track record. When asked if this was his idea of 'taking it easy,' Tom replied that he thought he had had quite a leisurely ride. The final score was Plymouth 16 Crystal Palace 37. In the second half Tom took on Plymouth's best rider, Bill Clibbett, in a match race. Unfortunately for the crowd, Clibbett's bike packed up and Tom continued on a solo run. Although he had no one to race against and didn't need to go all-out, his winning time was announced as 77.0 seconds, an incredible 1.4 seconds faster than the new track record he'd set earlier that evening.

The Glaziers' first home match was against one of the two remaining northern teams, Sheffield. Tom's first home ride of the season was in Heat 3 when he sped away from his opponents and won as he pleased. Mockford remarked after the race, 'Tom simply cannot go slow.' He then won his second race, also by a distance. However, taking things easy was not Tom's strong suit and in his third race, when once again in front of the opposition by an enormous distance, he fell on the last lap. Crystal Palace won the match 36–17. After two such convincing victories, the Glaziers were being spoken of as possible league champions.

Tom's challenge against Colin Watson in the BIC came the following week, preceding the league match against Plymouth. In the first heat, Watson won the toss and chose to take the inside position, but Tom rode round him on the first bend to establish a small lead. Watson then repassed him and was slightly ahead when he suffered engine failure, leaving Tom to complete the course alone. On the inside for the second heat, Tom put on the best display of riding ever seen at the Palace. He rode four perfect laps putting in a time of 77.0 seconds, 1.4 seconds faster than Joe Francis's track record set the week before. It was also claimed by the Crystal Palace management that this constituted a British record for a quarter-mile circuit. The fact that Crystal Palace's track was actually 449 yards shows just how remarkable this feat was.

In the match against Plymouth which followed, Tom won his first two heats, setting a new one-lap record on his way to winning Heat 3 when he was timed at 18.6 seconds for one lap. Unfortunately, after such

Tom in Crystal Palace colours at Belle Vue.

a magnificent meeting, Tom was injured in Heat 7 and had to be taken to hospital. As the riders got away at the start, Plymouth's Stan Lupton, who was inside Tom, drifted out towards the fence. Any other rider on the outside might have shut off, but this wasn't Tom's way and he tried to go through the narrow space left. As he did so he was squeezed into the fence and turned a terrifying somersault with his machine leaping into the air and landing on him. There was a deathly hush around the stadium as he was carried off on a stretcher and rushed straight to the Cottage Hospital. Fortunately the accident had looked much worse than it was and Tom was found to be suffering from nothing more than minor concussion. He was allowed home later in the afternoon.

Just over a week later, Tom met Watson in the second leg of their British Championship eliminator, this time at Watson's own track, Wembley. But it made little difference to Tom as he beat Watson easily in two straight runs, the first by at least 40 yards in a time just one-fifth of a second outside his own track record, while in the second he did slightly better, equalling his track record in a win by about the same distance.

He was now through to meet either Frank Arthur or Vic Huxley in the semi-final. Their long awaited clash had been twice postponed owing to bad weather, and when the first leg finally did take place it was as the precursor to Wimbledon's league match with Crystal Palace. In spite of these two top Australians being there that day, the *Speedway News* reported that 'the brightest of all the stars present that afternoon was Tom Farndon. He won every race in which he started, five in all.' Three were in the league match when he beat Huxley, and two in the second half scratch races, when he beat Huxley again as well as Claude Rye and Cyclone Billy Lamont.

Shortly afterwards, the teams for the First Test match at Stamford Bridge were announced and, for the first time, Tom was named in the team proper. Before the Test took place, Crystal Palace suffered some unexpected big losses, including one to Sheffield, a team they had beaten easily earlier in the season. One of the reasons for these losses was a return to the old days for Tom who began to suffer from engine problems again. With the Test match coming up, Tom put in extra time at the Crystal Palace workshops to make sure his machine was in a fit state to represent its country.

A crowd of something like 45,000 turned out to see England surprisingly beat Australia in the Test. Pre-match forecasts were generally to the effect that the Australians were too experienced for the England team and would win reasonably comfortably. One of the main reasons why these expectations were not fulfilled was the form of Tom Farndon. Accompanying the report of the Test in *Speedway News* was a full page photograph of Tom with the caption, 'Tom Farndon of Crystal Palace, the hero of the Test Match.'

Tom's first outing came in Heat 4 with the score at England 7 Australia 10. Tom's partner was Wembley's George Greenwood and their opponents were Vic Huxley and Lionel Van Praag. Tom paid little attention to the reputation of the Australian pair and was into the first bend ahead. From then on he gradually increased his lead, winning by a considerable distance. Behind him, his partner, after a bad start, managed to overtake both the Australians to give England a 5–1 and the lead, 12–11. By the time the pair came out again in Heat 7, England had once again fallen behind, but another 5–1, with Tom this time second to his partner, put them back in front. In their third heat together, it was Greenwood who went into an early lead but he fell coming out of the second bend leaving Tom in first place, but he was caught and passed by Billy Lamont. Tom soon regained the lead and stayed there to remain on (paid) maximum points. Heat 13 saw Tom once again win by a distance, this time over Lamont and Frank Arthur, to finish the match on 11 points and unbeaten by an opponent. Tom's performance undoubtedly helped secure England a deserved 50–41 victory on the night, and he certainly earned his 'hero' status in *Speedway News*.

Tom rounds his great rival Vic Huxley at Crystal Palace.

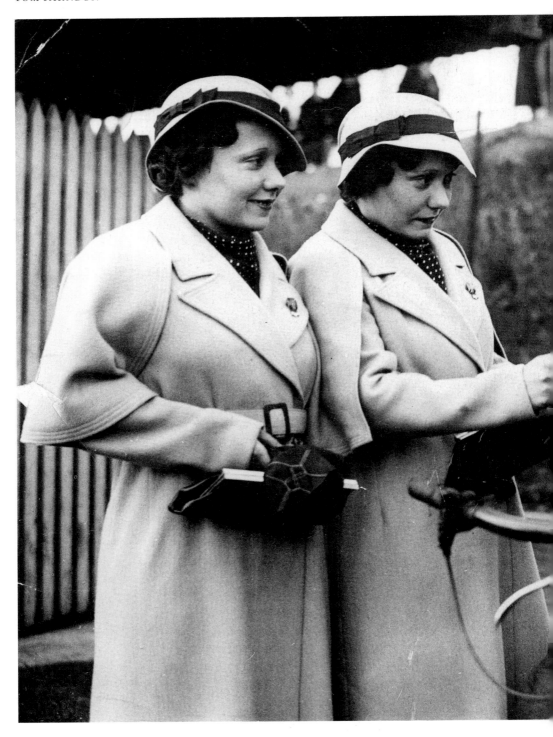

Tom with two of
his many female
admirers.

Shortly after the Test match the first set of league averages for the year were published. This showed Tom down in eleventh place with a cma of 8.00. Most of his dropped points, however, could be accounted for by engine failures and falls. Of the 27 races he finished, he had won 19.

Crystal Palace's next big test was an away match at Belle Vue. The Aces were equal first with Stamford Bridge at the top of the National League table and a very hard side to beat at home, with riders of the calibre of Frank Varey, Eric Langton, Max Grosskreutz and Joe Abbott. Of course, neither Belle Vue's reputation as a whole nor their riders as individuals fazed Tom. After a shaky start, falling in Heat 3 when in the lead, he went through the card unbeaten, defeating all four of Belle Vue's stars as he pleased and setting the fastest time of the night. Thanks to Tom and a magnificent performance by Joe Francis, the unthinkable happened and the strong Belle Vue team were defeated on their own track, 29–24.

Tom's old curse, machine problems, struck him hard in the Second Test match at Wembley. He failed to score a single point. On a number of occasions he was holding first or second place when his engine failed and he was left disconsolately pushing his bike back to the pits.

Meanwhile, Tom's pursuit of being named challenger for Parker's British Individual Championship continued with a 2–1 victory over Frank Arthur on Arthur's home track, Stamford Bridge. All three races were non-events as in each one the loser fell, leaving the victor to motor home alone. Nevertheless, it was a great victory for Tom. With the home leg to come, it now looked likely that he would progress to the final elimination round against Eric Langton.

The second leg took place on Saturday 18 June. The first race was all Tom. He trounced Arthur by 20 lengths. However, there was a shock in the second, Arthur winning by a similar distance. For the Crystal Palace faithful there was even more of a shock in the third race when Tom and Arthur were racing neck-and-neck for the lead, Tom fell, thereby handing the race and the second leg to his opponent.

The final and deciding leg was held at Plymouth the following Tuesday. Tom won the toss and elected to take the inside position. He took an early lead and managed to stay in front for three-and-a-half laps, with Arthur close behind and waiting for an error on Tom's part which would enable him to slip through. He must have thought his opportunity had gone when, uncharacteristically, Tom drifted just a little bit too wide on the final bend and Arthur was through like lightning to take the race in a new track record time of 76.1 seconds, 0.9 seconds faster than Tom's old one. After numerous delays including four false starts and then a stop for refuelling, Arthur got away well in the second race but could not keep the lead. Tom, with the sort of slide which would spell disaster for most riders, got inside Arthur and won in a time just one-tenth of a second slower than the new track record.

Tom sweeps round team-mates Harry Shepherd, centre, and Stan Greatrex, right.

The scene was all set for the deciding race. Tom won the toss and, in spite of the fact that the winner of the two previous races had come from the outside, chose the inside position. As they drove into the first bend, Tom fell and Frank, with nowhere to go, crashed into Tom and his fallen bike and also came down. A re-run was ordered; this time Arthur got away first. Tom tried to get through on the inside but hit Arthur's back wheel. He managed to stay on his bike but lost a considerable distance. It was noticeable that Tom was not quite himself following his fall and failed to ride with his usual dash in the decider. He did not put in the sort of pursuit that might have been expected of him and allowed Arthur to ease up and finish in the rather sedate time of 79.0 seconds.

Following his poor showing in the Test match and against Frank Arthur, Tom bounced back to form in the second-half events at Wembley two days later. In the final of the scratch race he beat home star Ginger Lees easily in a time of 79.8 seconds, the best time of the night. Then he defeated Lionel Van Praag in the first round of a special two-lap challenge competition in a time of 39 seconds, equalling Vic Huxley's record. In the final, Tom took the lead against Lees and Jack Ormston, but unfortunately overslid allowing Ormston to come through and win the race. He then attempted to beat the Wembley one-lap record of 19 seconds, but just missed out, recording 19.4. Nevertheless, in view of his recent misfortunes, this was a welcome return to form for Tom which was rewarded when the England Test selectors kept faith in him and picked him for the Third Test.

The National Speedway Association League finished in July with Crystal Palace taking third place behind Stamford Bridge and Wembley but 2 points in front of the strongly fancied Belle Vue team. Tom finished with a cma of 7.76 but had won 29 out of the 38 races in which he had finished. Taking out falls and engine failures, his cma was equal to 10.42, which gives a much better idea of his ability.

The first match in the new National League saw Crystal Palace take on West Ham at Custom House. Going into the final heat, the score was West Ham 22 Crystal Palace 23. The Glaziers therefore needed a 3–3 or better to win the match. Their two representatives in the last heat were Tom and Harry Shepherd, who so far had scored just one point between them all evening. It seemed odds-on for a West Ham victory, but when the fate of his side depended on him, Tom showed he was not a man to fail his team and he turned his evening's form upside down to lead from start to finish, ensuring Crystal Palace won the first match to be staged in the National League.

Tom put his disastrous performance in the Second Test match well and truly behind him, scoring 11 points in the third at Belle Vue, losing just once in his four races to Dick Case. And it was Tom who put England's victory beyond doubt. Coming into Heat 15 with two heats to go, the scores were England 44 Australia 40. Theoretically therefore, Australia still had a chance; but Tom destroyed it. He had a titanic struggle with Bluey Wilkinson who tried his best to keep the issue open until the last heat, but Tom got the better of him, ultimately winning rather easily to ensure victory for England. The final score was England 53 Australia 43.

Tom was naturally chosen for the Fourth Test on his home track of Crystal Palace but in Heat 4, his first ride, he fell on the first bend with his machine falling on top of him. He received medical attention on the track for a damaged leg and missed his next ride. He returned for his third ride but his injury was obviously having its effect as he trailed in a poor last. He recovered a bit of his form to finish behind his partner, Eric Langton, in his last ride, but it had not been a good night for Tom, scoring just 2 points and sustaining a leg injury.

Towards the end of August, Tom returned to his old stamping ground at Brandon where he recorded a fine maximum in the league match and then beat home side captain Syd Jackson in two straight runs in a best-of-three match race series. In spite of being the main cause of their 22–31 defeat and beating their captain in the second half, the Coventry fans gave Tom a rapturous reception as they still thought of him as 'their' man. Earlier in the season, when Tom beat Colin Watson to go through to the semi-finals of the British Individual Championship, the news was announced at Brandon as Coventry were racing that night and a great cheer had gone up from the crowd.

Tom followed up his maximum at Coventry with another fine performance, this time at home to Wimbledon, winning two races and suffering from engine failure when leading in his third. Although he was running into a bit of good form, Tom was surprisingly dropped to reserve for the fifth and final Test match at Wembley. However, George Greenwood was unable to take his place in the line-up and Tom was promoted to the team proper on the night. After a hesitant start, in which he trailed in last, Tom showed that he was worthy of his place by dropping just one point to an opponent in his last three rides, finishing with a score of 7, paid 8.

Tom's next big night was the final of the Star Riders' Championship. As in 1931, all teams were allowed two riders in the final, one to come through a qualifying process at their own track, the other to be nominated by the club. Crystal Palace had held its own round earlier in the year. The final had brought together the three crowd favourites, Ron Johnson, Joe Francis and Tom, and was eagerly anticipated by the fans. Disappointingly for them, Tom fell on the first bend but the other two raced neck-and-neck until Johnson overslid on the last corner of the last lap. Although he corrected the slide, he had lost too much ground and Francis went on to win, becoming Crystal Palace's first Star finalist. The club's other finalist was chosen by the popular vote of the supporters and was won by Tom.

The Wembley final took place on 22 September and Tom's first-round ride was in Heat 6. He was up against Wembley's own Ginger Lees, who was drawn on the outside, and Plymouth's Bill Clibbett. Tom got away first but a neat bit of work saw Lees cut back inside the pair and go on to win comfortably. The format of the Star Riders' Championship meant that only one rider went through to the next round, so Tom's evening was over.

And that was more or less it for Tom's 1932 season. There were a few more league matches but no more major honours to be ridden for. At the end of the National League season Tom finished with a cma of 8.27. Without taking the speedway world by storm Tom had consolidated his position as one of England's leading riders and was now recognised as a regular in the England Test team.

In spite of his many successes on the track in 1932, however, Tom would no doubt have felt his greatest accomplishment of the year was marrying

England v. Australia third
Test match, Belle Vue,
6 July 1935. From left to
right Lionel Van Praag and
Bluey Wilkinson lead for
Australia. Behind them on
the outside, Bill Kitchen is
just in the process of falling
while Tom tries to make up
ground on the inside.

his teenage sweetheart, Audrey Gledhill, at the Register Office in Little Park Street, Coventry, on 30 August after a year's engagement. The reason for getting married in a Register Office was that Audrey was very shy and didn't want to be married in a traditional white wedding gown in a church ceremony because she didn't want any fuss.

Audrey was very supportive of Tom's speedway career, accompanying him to most of his matches. Like Tom she was also a very keen dancer and they would go out dancing on many evenings. They even entered dancing competitions and were successful on a number of occasions. As Tom became more famous he began to be mobbed by girls both at the track and at the dance halls, but he didn't take any notice of them as he was devoted to Audrey.

After they were married they moved into a house called The Glade on the Bondi Carpio Manor Estate in Shirley, Surrey, to be near the Crystal Palace track. Tom hated housework and Audrey would get up at about four o'clock in the morning, do all the washing, get it cleared away and get everything spick and span before Tom came down for breakfast.

7

KING OF THE SPEEDWAY WORLD

(Crystal Palace, 1933)

He had been threatening to break through into the realms of speedway superstardom all season and now he had well and truly arrived.

Tom did not repeat his trip to the Antipodes during the winter, preferring instead to stay at home with his new bride and take in the South London dance halls. Before the season started, Fred Mockford announced the line-up for the 1933 Crystal Palace team which, naturally, included Tom.

A big change to occur in the speedway world at the start of 1933 was the abolition of the rolling start and the introduction of the standing start for league, cup and Test matches. Under the old rolling start method, the four riders had to come out of the pits, ride one lap and then come up to the line together at approximately 15 mph as the flag fell for the race to start. In spite of a number of changes to the starting procedure, the rolling start was still giving rise to a number of problems with many false starts and many races having to be restarted. The new method meant that riders no longer had to ride one lap of the track, but would come to the line and stop. Riders would then make a clutch-start when the steward signalled with a green light instead of a flag. Rolling starts were still used for all match races including the British Individual Championship.

Tom's first meeting of the year was the Wimbledon Open Championship, held at the end of April. The format for this event was that it was run off in two sections of seven riders. In each section, every rider met every other rider in three-man heats, with the winner of each section meeting in the final. Tom got off to a shaky start in Section A, losing to Wally Kilmister in the first heat, but he then won his next two heats to finish on 8 points. Tiger Stevenson also

Crystal Palace 1933. Left to right: Triss Sharp, Joe Francis, Nobby Key, Fred Mockford (co-promoter), Ron Johnson (captain), Tom, Harry Shepherd, George Newton.

finished on 8 points in the same section so a run-off was held to determine the winner. Tom won this comfortably, earning the right to meet the winner of Section B, Ginger Lees, in the final. Lees drew the inside berth and was off like a flash. Tom was left floundering in his wake and Lees won by a distance in the best time of the night. Although it was a disappointing end for Tom it was a good start to the season and he had taken some notable scalps in the meeting, including Tiger Stevenson, Vic Huxley and Norman Parker.

Back at Crystal Palace for his first home match of the season, however, Tom did not fare so well. He managed just 2 points, one second place, in his team's 28–33 loss to Wimbledon. This was followed by another measly two-point haul, away at West Ham. Even when Crystal Palace managed a thumping 41–22 win over the Hammers at home, Tom managed to contribute only 4 points.

After another poor showing at Wembley, Tom's season suddenly changed. He came right back to form with 10 points against Wimbledon (race winners received 4 points in 1933) and a paid maximum against Sheffield. Towards the end of May, following a further 6 points from two rides at home to Clapton, Tom shocked the Crystal Palace management by putting in a transfer request. Mockford was already having problems with one of his other star riders, Nobby Key. Key was being threatened with suspension by the Control Board for refusing to sign a new contract introduced by the board in 1933 for riders spending their winter abroad. It was part of an attempt to introduce a form of rider control so that some teams did not get too powerful. Accordingly it was announced that any rider not in the country over the close season, even if they appeared on a team's retained list, would become the property of the Control Board and could be allocated to any team on their return. As Key had spent the winter in Australia, he came in to this category and he was asked to sign a new contract by the Control Board. Key was not happy about this as he wished to stay at Crystal Palace and refused to sign the new contract. He was given until the end of May by the Control Board to sign or face suspension. With Tom choosing this moment to put in his transfer request, Mockford was now faced with losing his top two riders from the 1932 season.

Tom specifically requested a move to Wembley but Mockford refused the request on two grounds. The first was that he did not want him to leave at all. The second was that, even if he did leave, he thought Wembley would be far too strong with Tom in their line-up. If he really wanted to leave, Mockford said he would allow him to go back to Coventry or any of the other weaker provincial tracks. The Control Board agreed and refused Tom's request to move to Wembley. With that move ruled out, Tom agreed to stay at Crystal Palace because he did not wish to leave London.

While discussions on his future were going on, Tom did not ride for the Glaziers and missed the match at Plymouth, but he came back with a bang for the home match against Coventry on 3 June with his first full maximum of the season.

It was at about this time that Tom bought the bike he had been after for some time. He had long coveted a machine owned by Arthur Warwick of Stamford Bridge, and with Warwick's retirement Tom was able to secure it for a knockdown price. Once in possession of the bike he had long wanted to own, Tom made some alterations. One in particular caused some controversy at the time. This was a massive bar which stood out several inches from the left-hand side and on a level with the centre of the clutch. Some riders thought this a cunning device designed to slide along the track to prevent Tom from falling when he laid his machine over to take the corners. There were those who suggested that the Control Board should prohibit it. Tom's explanation was that it prevented the frame from twisting and protected his clutch on those occasions when he did fall off. He further claimed tests had proved that when the machine was inclined to the left, the handlebar touched the ground before the bar.

Although the new clutch-start introduced at the beginning of the season was designed to end the problems caused by false starts, the system still wasn't working very well as riders were still edging forward and trying to anticipate the start. To overcome this, Fred Mockford, together with Harry Shepherd, had been working on a new starting technique aimed at cutting out the recalled starts and the disqualifications. Borrowed from horse racing, it was an extremely simple idea consisting of a frame extended across the track with three horizontal tapes which rose as an operator pulled a handle. Along with his team-mates, Tom took part in these experiments and was therefore one of the first riders in the world to experience the starting gate. There were no springs and no complicated machinery of any kind to go wrong, the motive power being supplied by gravity through the medium of a weight. Before the experiment took place there was a fear that the riders would continually breast the tapes and the starting gate would prove to be no better than any other system in preventing false starts. However, the starting method that was employed stopped this happening because the riders had to line up a foot behind the gate with their engines running and their clutches out and start as soon as the tapes rose. Because of the speed of the tapes rising, no one was able to anticipate the start to such an extent that the tapes were broken at any

Tom, left, helps test the new starting gate.

time. It was claimed that the presence of something tangible in front of them prevented the riders from jumping off before the tapes rose and all the riders who took part in the experiment spoke strongly in favour of the starting gate. Although the experiment was an undoubted success, fears were expressed that speedway riders were such an ingenious lot that it would not be long before they found a way to anticipate the tapes and still manage to get flyers. On 17 June, in the second half of the match against Nottingham, the starting gate made its first public appearance.

In spite of the doubts, the Control Board announced at its meeting the following Tuesday that it had been so impressed by the results of the experiment at Crystal Palace, it had decided the starting gate was to be installed at all tracks for the purpose of clutch-start racing within three weeks of the date of the notice, and that from then on its use was obligatory in all official fixtures, although still not in match races. The only difference to the Crystal Palace experiment was that riders were to line up two feet behind the gate instead of one foot. Any rider touching the tapes would be sent back and, if they repeated the offence, they would be excluded from the race. The Control Board added that they couldn't see any reason why all tracks should not be able to install them within three weeks as the cost of constructing the gate was less than £5 including labour charges.

Despite his somewhat patchy form at the beginning of the season, Tom was chosen for the Probables in the England Test Trial match. But his place in the team for the First Test was left in some doubt after he managed only 7 points from six rides, and for the second trial at Clapton he was dropped to the Possibles. However, he fared much better in this meeting, top scoring with 20 points after a hurried dash from a league match at Crystal Palace. The earlier match had also seen him in good form, winning two heats against a Nottingham side.

With a total of 11 points away at Wimbledon, Tom was now getting back into the form that had made him one of the top riders the year before, a fact confirmed by his part in Crystal Palace's 39–23 rout of Wembley the following week in which he scored 10 points.

At the end of June, Tom became a film star when he doubled for Gordon Harker in *Britannia Of Billingsgate*. Part of the film, which had a speedway theme, was shot at Lea Bridge speedway and included Claude Rye, Arthur Warwick, Colin Watson, Gus Kuhn and Ron Johnson. But, in spite of these star names, it was Tom, because of his spectacular style, who was chosen to double for the leading man.

With 20 points in the second Test trial, Tom secured his place in the First Test match which took place on 29 June. However, a couple of crashes resulted in him missing his last three rides and he scored only 1 point. The solitary point

The England Test team at Wimbledon, 1933. From left to right: Bob Harrison, Joe Francis, Jack Parker, Syd Jackson, Tom, Ginger Lees, Bill Kitchen, Tiger Stevenson.

came in Heat 1 when he took Lionel Van Praag on the last bend to snatch third place behind Tiger Stevenson and Vic Huxley. In his second ride he was fighting a terrific duel with Bluey Wilkinson behind Ron Johnson, when he bumped Wilkinson and forced him on to the centre green. Wilkinson rode on the grass for a few yards and then returned to the track in front of Tom, who pulled up. His last race of the evening was Heat 8. He got away slowly but, because he was behind, decided to throw discretion to the winds and went all out to catch the third man, Jack Sharp. Unfortunately he touched Sharp's wheel, flew off his bike and landed awkwardly on the track. He was reported to be suffering from concussion and took no further part in the match.

In spite of his concussion, Tom was back in the saddle two days later for a home league match against Plymouth. His fall couldn't have done him much harm as he scored a full maximum and then went on to beat Tiger Stevenson in a special two-lap match race in the second half.

A London Cup tie against Wimbledon was next, and once again his contribution was invaluable. Crystal Palace took the first leg 65–60 at Wimbledon's own track. With one heat to go, the Glaziers were actually leading by 10 points with Tom having contributed 12 to the total. But the match ended on a bit of a comedy note. Tom and his partner, George Newton, were leading coming out of the second bend and looked set to increase their team's lead to 15, but Newton accidentally rammed his footrest under Tom's exhaust pipe bringing them both to a standstill firmly locked together. Tom was just extricated in time to avoid being lapped by the Wimbledon pair and managed to take third place, but it meant that Crystal Palace, instead of increasing their lead, actually found it halved to 5 points.

Tom's good form continued with 10 points at Sheffield, 14 in the return London Cup leg against Wimbledon and 10 away at West Ham. In spite of this good run, Tom was dropped to reserve for the Second Test at Belle Vue and did not get a ride.

With the Third Test being at Crystal Palace, Tom was back in the team. On this occasion he had a much better time of it. The match had been in danger of being called off because there had been heavy rain in the morning. Although the track was very heavy the decision was taken to go ahead. The state of the track didn't seem to worry Tom who rode magnificently in the first heat to win from his partner Ginger Lees, Vic Huxley and Ernie Evans in what was to turn out to be the fastest time of the day. Tom followed up this success with a win over his Crystal Palace captain Ron Johnson in his second race by a large margin. A third place just inches behind Huxley in Heat 10 was followed by a paid second in Heat 15 when he team-rode with Lees to keep out Dick Case and Max Grosskreutz. Tom's only last place came in his final race when he finished behind Johnson and Bluey Wilkinson. In spite of this he had a good afternoon, scoring 11 points.

When the first set of league averages was produced at the end of June, Tom was in sixth place with a cma of 8.91 (after converting four points for a win to three). He was some way ahead of the second Crystal Palace rider, Joe Francis. Top of the averages was Tom's old Coventry team-mate, Jack Parker, with a converted cma of 10.00.

Crystal Palace's next match was away at runaway leaders Belle Vue. However, thanks to Tom, the Aces didn't have it all their own way. He won his first race, beating Bob Harrison, and came third behind his partner, George Newton, in his second. The score with one heat to go was Belle Vue 30 Crystal

Tom at Crystal Palace in 1933.

Palace 26. Tom and Newton were out in the last heat and with just 4 points in it there was still a chance for an upset result. As the tapes went up, Belle Vue's Joe Abbott and Bill Kitchen left the Crystal Palace pair standing, but Tom gradually wore them down and, riding magnificently, managed to pass both of them. Newton, however, could not emulate his partner, finishing last. It was a close run thing and Tom had given Belle Vue fans a real fright.

Crystal Palace's next home meeting featured their round of the Star Riders' Championship. This time, instead of the supporters having a vote, the two representatives would be the first two men home in the final. Tom won his first heat from Joe Francis by a distance and then did the same in the final, beating Ron Johnson, Harry Shepherd and George Newton. So, under the new qualification rules, Tom and his captain were through to the Star Championship Final.

Tom returned to his old track Coventry the next day and scored the only maximum of the match, helping his team to an impressive 34–26 away victory. Four days later, he was back in Test action. Although the match itself was said to be 'most uninteresting' consisting of procession after procession, Tom once again acquitted himself well, scoring 11 points.

The only team that had any chance of overhauling Belle Vue for the league title was Wimbledon. They went down to Crystal Palace at the end of August hoping to keep their title challenge alive. Instead, what they got was a mauling of gigantic proportions, going down 46–17. Tom was in the forefront of this debacle scoring yet another impressive maximum, beating the likes of Vic Huxley and Syd Jackson with consummate ease.

The final Test match of the season was held at West Ham. The score was 2–2, so this was vital in deciding who would win the 1933 series. Tom, now in the form of his life, was once again chosen and did his part in ensuring a 74–52 victory for England. His first race came in Heat 2 and, as the tapes went up, he leapt to the front and won as he liked with the Australians nowhere. His old bugbear returned in Heat 4 when he suffered an engine failure. In his third ride Tom overslid on a bend but, as he so often was able to do, he raised his machine upright through pure strength, although this time his luck was out; the engine had stalled so he was unable to continue. His next outing was in Heat 13. From the tapes he and his partner, Colin Watson, led the Australian captain Vic Huxley. But as Huxley tried to get in between them, Watson hit a bump on the surface and found himself and his bike spreadeagled across the track. The race was stopped in the interests of safety. In the re-run, Tom took the lead straight away and remained there, winning by some 15 lengths. Tom's final race was the last heat of the night. By this time the match was all over and the race was pretty much a procession, Dick Case taking first place in front of Tom. In total he scored

10 points from five rides, but in two of those rides he did not finish. It was another fine performance.

His next meeting, a home match against West Ham, resulted in a minor riot when a group of spectators invaded the Palace Pavilion following a disputed last heat. What had happened was that, with one heat to go, the score was 29–26 in favour of the Glaziers. With the on-form Tom and George Newton representing Crystal Palace, it seemed odds-on for a home victory, even against West Ham's best and most formidable pairing, Bluey Wilkinson and Arthur Atkinson. As the gate was pulled down, one of the two tapes (one was missing) was seen to be hanging down. When the gate went up, the loose tape caught round Newton's neck. Tom, under the impression that a restart would be ordered, sat still. However, the steward let the race go, allowing Wilkinson and Atkinson to romp home for an easy victory, giving them a 6–1 and the match by 2 points.

There was pandemonium in the stadium and Fred Mockford announced that he had to accept the decision for the time being. This statement incensed a section of the crowd even more and a group of about thirty supporters broke into the Pavilion and demanded the blood of their own manager for giving in. Order was only restored when Mockford made a further announcement that he had already put in an official protest. The steward's excuse for allowing the race to continue was that from his position in the rostrum he could not see the tapes properly and was unaware that one was missing and that one was loose and caught round Newton's neck.

After their next meeting, the Control Board issued a statement which said, 'The Speedway Control Board have considered the Crystal Palace protest against the start of the last heat of their league match against West Ham on Saturday last, and have decided that the operation of the starting gate in that race was not in accordance with the regulations and the best interests of the sport. They consider that in fairness to the two teams there is no alternative but to declare last Saturday's match null and void and that it be replayed at the earliest opportunity.' The re-run didn't do Crystal Palace any good. They again lost, this time by the even narrower score of 32–31.

Tom's last meeting before the final of the Star Riders' Championship was a league match away at Wimbledon. He took the opportunity to stamp his authority by scoring a magnificent maximum, beating Vic Huxley, Syd Jackson and Gus Kuhn on their own track. Tom was now riding at the top of his form and one of the favourites to take the Star title.

The final of the Star Riders' Championship was held on 14 September at Wembley's Empire Stadium. Twenty of the best riders in speedway, two from each National League team, lined up for this prestigious event, then the equivalent of the World Championship.

Tom's first-round ride was against Norman Parker, Walter Moore and Frank Varey. Parker fell early on and Tom beat Moore and Varey by a distance. His time was only three-fifths of a second outside the track record, which, considering he had an untroubled ride, was quite remarkable. Tom then met Les Wotton in the first semi-final. Wotton had actually beaten Tom's time in his first-round ride by two-fifths of a second so it looked as though Tom was in for a real race this time. Also in the race were Eric Langton and Harry Whitfield. Tom made a brilliant start, and Wotton was last away. By the end of the second lap, Wotton had passed the other two and was chasing after Tom, but Tom was far too fast for him and he came home some 12 lengths in front.

Tom was now in the final against Ron Johnson and West Ham's Bluey Wilkinson. As the tapes went up, Tom and Wilkinson got away together and for two laps they literally fought for the lead. There was no quarter asked and none given. Gradually however, Tom began to edge in front and by the third lap had taken a substantial lead. Behind him, Wilkinson lost a tyre and had to retire. The championship now belonged to Tom. He had finally fulfilled his potential and was at last crowned Star Riders' Champion 1933.

Many commentators said after the meeting that it was definitely the best Star Championship final they had seen and probably the most exciting meeting ever to take place at Wembley. Tom thoroughly deserved his victory. He had been threatening to break through into the realms of speedway superstardom all season and now he had well and truly arrived. His victory was due to a combination of three things. He started faster than anyone else, he was faster during the race than anyone else and his control of the bike throughout was superb. He never once looked to be in any trouble. At twenty-three, Tom Farndon was king of the speedway world.

Two days later, he reaffirmed his class when he was instrumental in Crystal Palace's heavy defeat of league champions Wembley 42–21, scoring a faultless maximum and then going through the second half unbeaten to win the Palace Handicap. Tom's next two matches were home and away league fixtures against Plymouth. In the first, at home, he scored another maximum, while in the away match he had to give best in one race to Plymouth's Jack Sharp, winning his other two with some ease. Next was a home match against Belle Vue, which saw Tom back to his maximum best, beating riders of the class of Bill Kitchen, Max Grosskreutz, Eric Langton and Frank Varey. Heat 4 in particular showed Tom at his most brilliant as he took on Langton and Varey who were generally reckoned to be the best pair riding in speedway at the time, and one of the greatest partnerships of all time. As the race started they outgated Tom, and once in front these two were very rarely defeated. But Tom stayed right behind them for two laps and after making two or three good attempts to drive between them, he finally made it on the first bend of lap three. All three rode almost line abreast until the first bend of the last lap. At that point Tom took the lead and held it to a close finish.

In the second half he took part in a special challenge match race in which promoter Fred Mockford had to complete two laps against Tom's three. Even with an extra lap to race, Tom lost by just four lengths. That same day, Crystal Palace travelled across to Clapton for an away fixture and, although Palace lost the match, Tom scored another maximum, making two maximums in one day.

Vic Huxley leads Tom at Lea Bridge.

Tom, left, takes on Crystal Palace co-promoter Fred Mockford, right, in a special challenge match race in which Mockford had to complete two laps against Tom's three. Even with an extra lap to race, Tom lost by just four lengths.

The final few weeks of the season had confirmed Tom's place as probably the best speedway rider in the world. In spite of a fairly average start to the season he finished it in sixth place in the averages with a cma of 9.56, having recorded nine full and one paid maximum. His form towards the end of the year was nothing short of stunning. Not only did he win the Star Riders' Championship but he also scored five of his nine maximums between 11 September and 7 October in just seven matches.

Although it was now coming to the end of the season, there was some sensational news still to come from promoters Fred Mockford and Cecil Smith. Visitor numbers to the Crystal Palace grounds were in general decline and the only two attractions that were still regularly pulling in large numbers were motorcycle path racing and speedway. The trustees of the Palace felt they needed to make their money out of these and consequently proposed a dramatic increase in rent to something like £1,000 per week. This, combined with their refusal to sanction floodlights at the speedway track, forced the promoters to seriously consider their future at Sydenham. On 13 October it was announced that Messrs Mockford and Smith had completed negotiations to lay down a brand new track at New Cross stadium, and would transfer their operation there at the start of the 1934 season. The team, including Tom, was to remain essentially the same.

8

CELEBRITY STATUS

(New Cross, 1934)

Hero worship of this charismatic figure was now reaching proportions that formerly only footballers and film stars could hope to aspire to. He became the most popular speedway rider ever.

Before the season started there was a very happy event in the Farndon household as Audrey gave birth to their son, Roy. Tom now had another mouth to feed and he was more determined than ever to rise to the very top of his profession.

The move to New Cross entailed a complete change of riding condition. Whereas Crystal Palace was one of the longest tracks in the country at 449 yards, New Cross was the shortest at 262 yards, giving rise to its nickname, the Frying Pan. It was of great interest to the speedway world to see if the new Star Champion could adapt to the different circumstances in which he now found himself.

The opening fixture at New Cross on 18 April, a match against West Ham, attracted 15,000 spectators. Tom answered any questions there may have been about his ability to adapt by not only scoring a maximum, but also setting the fastest time of the night, 63.0 seconds, which became the first official track record. He had begun 1934 as he finished 1933 and firmly established himself as the favourite not only with the old supporters he brought with him from Crystal Palace but also with a completely new set of fans at New Cross.

Along with the change of track it was felt a new nickname was required as the Glaziers was no longer appropriate. In the programme for the opening night, Fred Mockford wrote, 'Of course we have not yet got a nickname for the team, but we naturally think you would soon find one. One of our supporters wrote in to me the other day and suggested that as our track is between Canterbury Road and the Den (Millwall's Football Ground), a most suitable name would be "The Lambs"; just think of the war cry. "Baa! Baa! Baa!"' The

The proud parents, Tom and Audrey show off baby Roy.

name, the Lambs, stuck and that's how the team were known until 1936 when a new nickname, the Tamers, came in to being.

The first official away match saw New Cross given the toughest possible task. It was away to the runaway 1933 champions Belle Vue, but thanks to Tom the newcomers gave the champions the shock of their lives running them to a single point, just losing 26–25. He was easily the fastest rider on show that night. In his winning ride against Eric Langton and Frank Varey he clocked a time of 80.6 seconds, almost two seconds faster than any time any of the home riders could manage to put up. Going in to the last heat of the match the scores were Belle Vue 24 New Cross 21. Tom and Harry Shepherd were out for the Lambs. With the Aces just needing not to lose 5–1 (scoring was back to 3-2-1) to ensure victory, the Belle Vue pairing just allowed Tom to go. They knew there was no stopping him that evening and they concentrated their efforts on trying to keep Shepherd from taking second place.

Three nights later, New Cross were away at Birmingham. For once Tom had to give best in a race, losing to Les Wotton in Heat 9, but he did have the satisfaction of breaking the Birmingham track record in Heat 3.

Tom once more delighted his home crowd scoring another maximum in the next match against Harringay, helping New Cross to a 29–25 win. The *Speedway News* reported that, 'The local hero is Tom Farndon. Never did a star footballer receive more wholehearted applause from

Tom in New Cross colours.

South-East London than did Tom Farndon after he had won his third heat and the match for New Cross. He combines the spectacular with the effective.'

The next two meetings, away at Plymouth and home to Birmingham, brought two more maximums for Tom and by the end of April he was sitting on top of the National League Averages, with a cma of 10.67. His nearest rival was Vic Huxley with 10.34 and it was Huxley who was to inflict on Tom his next defeat in an away fixture at Wimbledon. After losing to Huxley, Tom returned to his winning ways scoring maximum after maximum throughout May. On 29 May not only did he score a maximum away at West Ham, but in the last heat of the match he smashed the track record.

The month was climaxed by the London Riders' Championship held at New Cross. The format was for 18 heats consisting of three riders per heat, each of whom rode three times on a points basis of 2-1-0, with the three highest scorers going in to the final. Tom won all three of his first round races, including a magnificent win over Vic Huxley.

Tom was joined in the final by Huxley and Ginger Lees. The draw saw Huxley on the inside, Tom in the middle and Lees on the outside. As the tapes went up, Tom was away like lightning. The others had no chance of catching the home track hero who went on to win by at least 20 yards. The fans' adulation of their idol reached new heights. The ovation that greeted Tom's victory was said to be the longest and loudest ever accorded a speedway rider in the history of the sport.

Hero-worship of this charismatic figure was now reaching proportions that formerly only footballers and film stars could hope to aspire to. The whole of south-east London seemed in thrall to this man as he became the most popular speedway rider ever. Not only was Tom almost unbeatable, but he was one of the most spectacular riders around, still keeping to the old leg-trailing style, and having the horrifying habit of flinging his machine over on the bends so far that in most races his knee was brushing the track. He was then, by sheer physical strength, able to haul it upright again. He could ride inside or outside, hug the white line or scrape the fence, whichever seemed the best way at the time. His physical strength stemmed from the fact that he was a non-smoker and teetotal and was always in the peak of condition. He was one of the few riders who could ride four laps and then come in without showing the slightest sign of the terrific exertion and strain he had undergone. To add to his appeal, Tom was one of the most modest sportsmen around. He was said to be the only rider who would rather blame himself rather than his machinery if he did not win a race. And, as if that wasn't enough, he had all the good looks and charm of a Hollywood celebrity as well.

Tom put his new-found success down to the fact that he had at last given up worrying about his own bikes, leaving them to his mechanic. In that way he was able to forget all about speedway in between meetings, concentrating more on greyhound racing which he had now taken up with a passion. He felt this made him approach each meeting in a fresh frame of mind. His view was that a rider who devoted all his time to tuning his machines had so many worries about what might happen to them that when the time came for riding them he couldn't give his undivided attention to the racing itself.

Naturally, Tom was chosen for England in the year's first Test match at Wembley. In his first race he carved a whole second off the Wembley track record. Apart from this spectacular start however, he had a fairly ordinary meeting for him, scoring just 8 points, twice losing to his big rival Vic Huxley. Back in league action, Tom continued to knock up big scores, with maximums against Wimbledon at home and Plymouth away, eight against Belle Vue and seven away at Harringay. The Second Test match was on Tom's home track and once again he broke the track record. This time he had to do it the hard

Tom with his beloved greyhounds.

way. He got a poor start and was shut out at the first bend behind Ron Johnson and Bluey Wilkinson. However, he managed to catch and pass both of them to record 61.4 seconds, beating Eric Langton's track record by 0.2 seconds. He now held the four-lap clutch-start record at five National League tracks.

Tom's inclination to break track records wherever he went led to a popular joke in speedway circles at the time which went something like this, 'A little boy staggered across the room with a huge parcel. His mother appearing in the doorway watched him anxiously, afraid to cry out in case he should drop it in fright. Bearing up bravely under its weight, he reached the edge of the gramophone cabinet; another step and he could place it on the shelf. Then, catching his foot in the carpet, he fell! "Oh, Tom!" cried his mother, "you've broken all the records again!"'

Tom's next two outings for New Cross were in the first round of the National Trophy. Although league matches were still run over nine heats, giving each rider three rides each, National Trophy matches were run over 18 heats with six rides per rider. The first leg was away at West Ham. Tom dropped just one point to Tommy Croombs in a thrilling race. Back home at New Cross, he went through the card undefeated. His 35 out of a possible 36 points in both legs ensured New Cross's progression through to the semi-finals.

By the end of June, in spite of his continued good run, Tom had dropped to second place in the averages behind Huxley who had a cma of 10.52 compared with Tom's 10.40. This probably says more about Huxley's form at the time than it does about any loss of form Tom might have been suffering. Some way behind, in third place, was Dick Case on 9.78. Huxley's scintillating form in 1934 had enabled him to regain his British Individual Championship, having lost it at his first defence back in 1931. Over two legs in May, he had beaten the then holder, Tiger Stevenson, to regain the championship without losing a race. It was inevitable that the Control Board would nominate Tom as Huxley's first challenger, given the dominance of the two men.

Tom's preparation for the match race series included taking part in the New Cross Supporters' Club outing to Dymchurch on 22 July. Such was the demand for places when it was known that Tom would be joining the outing, that no fewer than twenty-three coaches were booked. He was surrounded by his fans all day, except for once when the crowd seemed to think it would be good fun for Tom to take a dip in the sea fully dressed. At that point he showed that he didn't always need a motorcycle to move fast and his hundred yards dash off the beach was thought to have broken all records.

In what was to be a great confidence boost for Tom, his last meeting before the championship was a Best Pairs Trophy at Harringay, two nights before. Paired with Ron Johnson, they scored maximum points against the top pairs from West Ham, Lea Bridge, Harringay and Birmingham. The scene was now

Vic Huxley with his wife, Sheila.

set for the old maestro versus the young pretender, as many people saw it. Naturally there was a lot of press speculation about what the outcome would be, with Vic Huxley generally being spoken of as favourite to retain his title. Tom's manager, Fred Mockford, would have none of it however. Writing in the New Cross programme, he said:

> I was very annoyed the other day in reading Trevor Wignall's sports article in the *Daily Express*. He was talking about the British Individual Championship and finished up by saying that all the betting is in favour of Vic Huxley. Quite frankly, it seems almost incredible to me that a gentleman of his repute, writing in a leading London Newspaper, should insult the intelligence of his readers with such utter piffle. Surely to goodness he should be familiar with what he is writing about, and I can assure you that I, or any other promoter, would be only too pleased to give him all the information that he would require on Speedway matters.

The first leg was held at Huxley's track, Wimbledon, on 30 July. Tom won the toss and took the inside in the first race. He proved to be much too fast for Huxley. He was first away from the start and never looked likely to be beaten. In defeating Huxley in the first leg he also took away his track record, lowering it by three-fifths of a second to 69.8. In the second leg, Huxley managed to keep up with Tom as far as the first corner, but Tom, on the outside this time, went round Huxley as if he was standing still. Once again his time was 69.8. It was obvious a major new talent had arrived on the scene. Anyone who could

Vic Huxley, left,
shakes hands with
Tom before their
British Individual
Championship
contest.

beat the great Vic Huxley so easily and so convincingly on his own track must surely be the new number one of the sport.

The return leg at New Cross, two nights later on 1 August, was to see an even more sensational development in the rise of the new speedway superstar. As news spread around South London of Tom's performance at Wimbledon, crowds flocked to the Old Kent Road to see the sport's latest phenomenon, and it was in front of a 30,000 capacity crowd that Huxley won the toss and elected to take the inside position.

This time it was Huxley who got away first, and for almost two laps the Australian ace kept Tom at bay. But Tom was not to be denied and, going round the fourth bend of the second lap, he pulled out all the stops and rode a

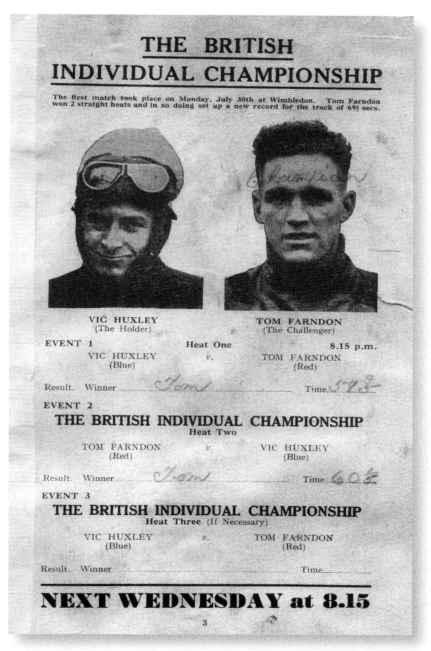

THE BRITISH
INDIVIDUAL CHAMPIONSHIP

The first match took place on Monday, July 30th at Wimbledon. Tom Farndon won 2 straight heats and in so doing set up a new record for the track of 69¼ secs.

VIC HUXLEY
(The Holder)

TOM FARNDON
(The Challenger)

EVENT 1   Heat One   8.15 p.m.

VIC HUXLEY   *v.*   TOM FARNDON
(Blue)   (Red)

Result. Winner ..... *Tom* ..... Time. *59.3*

EVENT 2

THE BRITISH INDIVIDUAL CHAMPIONSHIP
Heat Two

TOM FARNDON   *v.*   VIC HUXLEY
(Red)   (Blue)

Result. Winner ..... *Tom* ..... Time ... *60.5*

EVENT 3

THE BRITISH INDIVIDUAL CHAMPIONSHIP
Heat Three (If Necessary)

VIC HUXLEY   *v.*   TOM FARNDON
(Blue)   (Red)

Result. Winner ..... Time ...

NEXT WEDNESDAY at 8.15

3

The filled-in page from the New Cross programme of 1 August 1934 recording not only that Tom had beaten Vic Huxley to become the British Individual Champion but also the time of 59.6 seconds, the first time that any rider had completed four laps of a British speedway track in under one minute.

magnificent corner right round the boards passing Huxley as they came into the home straight. From then on he gradually pulled away, winning by eight lengths. Although this had been an exciting enough race in itself, which had brought the crowd to their feet, it was when the time was announced that there were loud gasps from the spectators. The time was 59.6 seconds, smashing the current record, held by Eric Langton, by an astonishing 1.4 seconds. It was the first time on any track in the country that the magic one minute mark had been beaten, albeit from a rolling start. The second leg was something of an anti-climax, Tom leading from start to finish and winning in 60.2.

In the following week's programme Fred Mockford had this to say:

> Congratulations, Tom, on a wonderful performance . . . I personally feel particularly proud of Tom's accomplishments. I suppose most of you, like myself, were tickled to death when you opened your *Daily Mail* on Thursday morning last and found Mr. Tom Webster's cartoon in respect of New Cross Speedway and Tom Farndon. Apart from being a great compliment to us, it is undoubtedly one of the best things in the way of publicity that has appeared in connection with the sport of Speedway Racing, and I feel that this cartoon has gone a long way to establishing Speedway Racing as a truly National Sport.

Tom had beaten the old champion, and the man generally reckoned at the time to be still the greatest speedway rider of all time, in four straight runs, on every occasion beating the old track record. He was now British Champion and the only rider ever to hold the Star Riders' Championship, the London Riders' Championship and the British Championship titles simultaneously. In some ways Tom's success also represented a symbolic change for British speedway – the old Australian master, the man who had dominated the early years of the sport in Britain, had been beaten by this young up-and-coming English rider.

Tom's achievement in taking the British Championship was the talk of speedway. One often forgotten fact in all of this was that on the night between the two legs, Tom rode in a league match at Birmingham. It might have been supposed that in view of what was happening he would take it a bit easy; but not Tom. He stormed to a perfect maximum, beating the likes of Jack Ormston and Les Wotton on their own track.

A week after he had become the British Individual Champion, Tom took part in his own club's qualifying round to find their two representatives for the Star Riders' Championship, the title he, of course, held. After winning his preliminary heat from Stan Greatrex, he took his place in the final alongside Ron Johnson, Joe Francis and George Newton. At the first attempt to start, Johnson burst through the tapes but, for some reason, was not excluded.

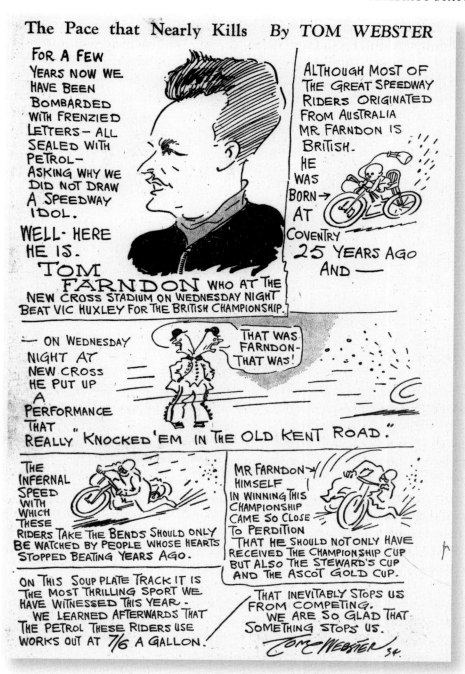

The Tom Webster cartoon that appeared in the *Daily Mail* on 2 August 1934 that Fred Mockford felt went 'a long way to establishing speedway racing as a truly national sport.'

Tom being presented with the British Individual Championship trophy by the Mayor of Deptford. On the left is the mayoress. Fred Mockford is in the centre and on the right is the famous aviator, Jim Mollison, husband of Amy Johnson, the even more famous aviator.

When, after a few more delays, the riders finally got away, Tom was hemmed in, filled up and fell on the first bend, leaving Johnson and Francis to take first and second places. Incredibly, Tom, arguably now the greatest rider currently riding, would not be at Wembley to defend his title.

In spite of this disappointment, Tom continued on his imperious way in the league, proving unbeatable at home and almost so away. During this period he also took the Cearns Trophy at Wimbledon, having tied with Bluey Wilkinson on 13 points and winning the run-off. The first challenger for his British title was his own captain, Ron Johnson. Because they were both New Cross riders, it was agreed that it would be decided over just one leg. That took place on 5 September.

The first of the three possible races was disappointing; Tom broke a chain on the second lap and Johnson rode home alone. The second required five attempts before it could be started. Johnson fell on the first bend and Tom stopped. Tom then pulled up with frame trouble and Johnson stopped. But the race, when it did finally come, was worth waiting for. The lead changed hands several times before the champion finally drew away to win by 10 lengths and carve a further 1.8 seconds off the track record, lowering it to 57.8 seconds. The third race was Tom all the way in a time also well inside the old track record, 58.6. Tom had now become the first man to successfully defend the British Individual Championship since the competition had begun. In the league match against Birmingham which followed, he scored yet another maximum. After this win, Tom's popularity reached even greater heights. He became a bit of a media star, making a fifteen-minute broadcast on national radio on 8 September.

Thanks to the twin spearhead of Tom and Ron Johnson, New Cross were having an excellent season and reached the final of the London Cup against West Ham. The first leg was held at New Cross on 19 September. As usual, the pair led the fight for the home team with paid 17 and 15 points respectively, Tom suffering a fall in his last race. The final score of 62–44 gave the Lambs an 18-point lead to defend at Custom House.

The return leg took place six days later. This was a much closer affair, with home riders Bluey Wilkinson and Tommy Croombs in particular taking the fight to their opponents. But New Cross lost by a solitary point, 53–52, giving them a 17-point victory on aggregate, 114–97. As well as winning the London Cup, the team also finished third in the league behind the recognised superteams of the sport, Belle Vue and Wembley.

Tom still had one more challenge to his individual title to fend off, this time from Belle Vue's Australian ace, Max Grosskreutz. The first leg was held at New Cross on 3 October. Much to everyone's surprise, Grosskreutz not only got the better of Tom in the first heat but also lowered his track record to 57.6 seconds. Tom came storming back in the second heat to force a decider, which turned out to be one of the best races seen at New Cross all season. Tom fought off his challenger's determined attempts to get past, taking the heat and the leg in yet another new track record time of 56.8 seconds.

The second leg was held on 6 October at Belle Vue and this time it was Grosskreutz's supporters turn to be surprised as Tom stormed to a first heat win over their home-track favourite in a time equalling the Belle Vue track record. Grosskreutz got his revenge by winning the next two heats. The overall score was now 1–1.

New Cross v Wembley.
Left to right: Lionel Van
Praag, George Newton,
Colin Watson, Tom.

Tom's Star Championship medals.

The deciding leg was held at Wembley on 11 October. The first two heats were won narrowly by the man on the inside, so when Grosskreutz drew the inside gate in the final and deciding heat, many thought Tom's reign as individual champion was over. Sure enough, Grosskreutz took the advantage going into and coming out of the first bend and held the lead until the final corner. But what happened then was later described by those lucky enough to witness it as the greatest piece of riding ever seen. Recalling the race many years later, Ron Johnson wrote, 'Max was in the middle of the last corner when Tom entered it. He drove his motor "flat" into and around the bend without moving an inch from the white line and won by half a wheel. I shouted myself hoarse from a seat in the grandstand. I have never seen any rider, before or since, handle a machine like Tom did that night.'

It was a classic manoeuvre and one that epitomised the sheer class and daring of the man, Tom's two outstanding qualities that had put him at the top of the speedway tree and made him the idol of the fans. He was now being mobbed wherever he went and had to be smuggled in and out of places through the back way, just like modern pop stars. The big stores used to borrow his trophies to display, and he never had to buy anything to wear, it was all given to him. He was treated like a major celebrity.

He finished the year with a cma of 10.06. Apart from falls and engine failures, Tom lost just four races to an opponent in 16 matches at home. Between 31 July and 15 August he scored four maximums on the trot, two at home, two away. In all, he scored fourteen full maximums and one paid maximum. During the year he became the only rider to hold the three

Max Grosskreutz.

New Cross, 1934. From left to right: Nobby Key, Tom, Ron Johnson, Fred Mockford, Harry Shepherd, Stan Greatrex, Roy Dook.

major individual trophies at the same time and also became the only man to successfully defend the British Individual Championship, which he did twice. His earnings from the championship alone had so far totalled £300, by today's values, the equivalent of almost £11,000.

In addition to winning the London Riders' Championship and the Cearns Trophy, 1934 had also seen Tom win the New Cross Ashes and the Goodwood Cup at Walthamstow. His smashing of track records all over the country was legendary. He held most of the National League track records including the one-lap flying start record at every single first division track.

Now at the peak of his form, Tom and his fans were looking forward to 1935 with great enthusiasm that it would once again be Tom's year and consolidate his place at the very top of the speedway world.

9

MYSTERY AND CONTROVERSY

(New Cross, 1935)

Dropped by England sensation – but why was the country's best rider left out of the First Test?

As if to underline Tom's place as Britain's number one speedway rider, the *Speedway News* featured his photograph on the front cover of their first edition of 1935. And just to further confirm his position, Tom opened the season by scoring a 9-point maximum in a challenge match away at Wimbledon, which included yet another great win over Vic Huxley.

Unfortunately, Tom did not have a very auspicious start to the season at his own track. In New Cross's first meeting, the Jubilee Cup, after a magnificent winning ride in his opening race, he blew his motor in his second and took no further part in the meeting.

Getting over this disappointment, Tom's next outing was at Harringay three nights later in a league match. Although New Cross were easily beaten 44–27 in a new 12-heat format introduced for league matches, Tom scored a maximum 12 points. He then travelled to West Ham for their opening meeting of the season, a Best Pairs contest. The crowd certainly got their money's worth in the first heat alone, when Tom and West Ham's own hero, Bluey Wilkinson, fought it out like a couple of scalded cats for the whole four laps. The race was only decided on the last bend, Tom riding inside Wilkinson to win by a length in the fastest time of the evening. Tom and his partner, Ron Johnson, went on to win the competition, scoring 22 points out of a possible 25 between them.

Tom was now getting well in to his stride and in his next meeting, the first home league match of the season, against West Ham, he scored another four-ride maximum. In the second half he broke the two-lap rolling start track record with a time of 29.6 seconds.

Not surprisingly, New Cross failed to win their next match away at Belle Vue, but, in front of a crowd of 23,000, it was said to have been one of the most exciting matches of all time, with passing and repassing in every heat and not one race that could be described as a procession. The final score of 41–30 to the Aces would most probably have been a bit closer had Tom not fallen victim to a strange refereeing decision in Heat 6. In that race he got a real flyer, ducking under the tapes to avoid breaking them and getting excluded. The normal practice in 1935 was to have a restart with all four back if this happened, but for some reason the steward decided to exclude the New Cross star. An appeal against the exclusion was later rejected by the Control Board.

In the next home meeting, Tom broke the one outstanding New Cross track record. He already held the four-lap rolling start record, the two-lap rolling start and the one-lap flying start. In the match against Hackney Wick on 1 May, he completed the set by taking the four-lap standing start record, then held by Jack Parker, with a time of 60.4. The race in which he did it showed Tom at his absolute best. It came in Heat 4 of the match. At the end of the third lap Tom was about half a length behind Hackney's Dick Case. Suddenly he shot past Case and went on to win by a large margin to record the first of his four wins in the match.

In the return fixture at Hackney Wick a few days later, Tom treated the fans to a piece of typical 'Farndonesque' riding in one heat when he overslid on the first bend and went broadside on to the track. He didn't quite fall off, however, and managed to right himself. He then chased after the other three, who by then were some way in front. To the growing cheers of the crowd he gradually caught them up and passed them all. Even the home supporters gave him a big cheer when he crossed the line in first place. Although this ride was typical of Tom, what was not so typical was that he actually lost a race, to Dick Case, in one heat and finished the meeting with 'only' 11 points.

Following the tremendous race Tom had with Bluey Wilkinson in the opening meeting at West Ham, their shrewd manager, Johnnie Hoskins, booked Tom to appear in the second half of the Hammers' next home meeting for a match race against Wilkinson. There was some confusion over whether this was to be run like the British Individual Championship with a best of three home and away, or whether it was just a one-off single race.

Before the pair met, the *Speedway News* ran an editorial which, although it praised the managements of both West Ham and New Cross for their astuteness, felt that this meeting would pre-empt Tom's next challenge for

Crystal Palace and New Cross co-promoter, Cecil Smith.

the official title. In their view, Wilkinson was one of the few men who stood any chance at all against him and it was likely therefore that he would be the next chosen challenger. By meeting before, the official meeting, when it came, would be robbed of a good deal of interest. They reported that, because of this very point, the Speedway Control Board had put its foot down and had ordered that the riders must meet for one heat only on each track, a decision with which *Speedway News* agreed.

Cecil Smith, the co-promoter at New Cross, responded to this by saying that it was only ever intended to be a one-off single match race to be held at West Ham and that at no time had either they or West Ham received any communication from the Control Board, nor were they likely to as they had not done anything wrong. After all the toing and froing in the press, the match race took place on 7 May. Tom swept away his opponent, winning easily in a new track record time, beating Vic Huxley's old record set up the year before.

In spite of the protestations of both the West Ham and New Cross managements that they were not intending to pre-empt the British Individual Championship itself, it may have been because of this loss at home that Wilkinson was not chosen as Tom's next challenger. This honour went instead to Hackney's captain, Dick Case. The dates were set for 5 June at New Cross and 7 June (Case's twenty-fifth birthday) at Hackney. The naming of these dates caused a great deal of controversy in the press because the day in between, 6 June, was an England v. Australia Test match. This was felt to be most unfair to the two men. In addition there was some criticism that the dates had been set so far in advance. The *Speedway News* in particular felt that the enthusiasm engendered by the announcement of the challenger and the dates would be dissipated by the time the races actually came round.

New Cross's next home meeting saw Dick Case, Joe Francis and Max Grosskreutz make attempts on Tom's 14.4 second flying start one-lap record. Case recorded 14.8, Francis 15.0 and Grosskreutz 14.4. Because Grosskreutz had equalled the record it was felt only fair to give Tom a chance as well. In a faultless ride he regained sole ownership of the record by coming home in 14.2 seconds.

Incredibly, Tom was left out of the England side for the 6 June Test match. This gave rise to a story that he had asked to be left out because it was in between the two match race challenges, but he flatly denied this. Cecil Smith told the press that Tom had never turned down an engagement on account of too much riding and that to say he was 'astonished at his omission from the first Test is to put it mildly.' Tom said that he never for one moment thought he would be left out and that he would be an automatic choice. He went on to say:

> I am riding better than ever this year. The only men who have really beaten me are Case and Huxley . . . All told, I suppose the number of times

For **RIDER**

Price 1/-
(IN TRIPLICATE)
Form S.R. 9

AUTO-CYCLE UNION

APPROVED FORM OF SPEEDWAY RIDER'S AGREEMENT

An Agreement made this _23rd_ day of _July_, 1935

BETWEEN _London Motor Sports Ltd_

(hereinafter called " The Promoter "), Promoter of meetings at the _New Cross_

1. Full Name.
2. Trade, Profession, or Occupation (if any) in which the rider is actively engaged in addition to Speedway Riding.
3. Address.

SPEEDWAY (hereinafter called " the Home Track ") of one part and (1) _Tom_

London, (2) _____, of (3) _Flat 11 Coombe Manor_

Estate – Monks Orchard – Shirley near Croydon

Competition Licence No. _35/605_ (hereinafter called " The Rider ") of the other part,
WHEREBY IT IS AGREED as follows :—

1. The Rider hereby warrants that he is not a party to any Agreement, Contract or other obligation which prevents his due performance of this Agreement.

2. The Rider shall attend and compete at such meetings on licensed tracks within England, ~~Scotland, Wales, ...~~ and including the thirty-first day of December, 1935, and the Rider shall not compete at any other meeting or in any other race without the consent in writing of the Promoter.

3. The Promoter shall, except in case of emergency, give the Rider not less than two nor more than fourteen clear days' notice in writing that the Promoter desires the Rider to compete at a particular meeting and by giving such notice shall impliedly warrant that the meeting is being held under the permit and the Speedway Regulations of the Auto-Cycle Union and upon a Track licensed by the Auto-Cycle Union, and the acceptance of such notice by the Rider shall impliedly warrant that the Rider undertakes to conform to the said regulations of the Auto-Cycle Union on his part.

4. The Rider hereby undertakes, on the signing of this Agreement, to provide at his own expense and for his exclusive use one motor-cycle specially constructed for Speedway Racing, mechanically perfect and in a fit and proper condition for racing. The Rider further undertakes to maintain the said motor-cycle in first-class racing condition throughout the period of this Agreement, unless he shall have entered into an agreement with the Promoter whereby the Promoter will maintain the motor-cycle in such condition at the Rider's expense.

5. The Rider shall be in the paddock, dressed and ready for racing not less than 15 minutes prior to the advertised time for the starting of the meeting, and shall not leave the paddock until after the last event on the programme except with the express permission of the Clerk of the Course or of the Chief Paddock Marshal. A Rider failing to carry out any of the terms of this Clause shall be so informed at the meeting, and unless he can explain such failure to the satisfaction of the Promoter, forfeit a sum not exceeding £2 out of the money due to him for the meeting.

6. The Rider shall be entitled to the following payments :—
   (a) A fee of 1s. (one shilling) on the signing of this Agreement.
   (b) Starting Money, Prize Money and Expenses in accordance with the Schedule herein.

All such Starting Money, Prize Money and Expenses shall be payable as follows :—
   (a) For all Events on the Home Track.
   (b) For League, Cup Tie and other Team Events on Away Tracks. } By the Home Track Promoter.

   (c) For other Events on Away Tracks. } By the Away Track Promoter.

Tom's 1935 New Cross contract.

I have been defeated this season could be counted on the fingers of one hand. The fact that I am somewhere near the top of the point-scoring list is sufficient indication of that. I took it so much for granted that I would be in the team that I have spent all the past week or so getting two motors ready – one for the Test and the other for my match race with Case. Personally, I think my omission rather spoils my meeting with Dick. If I beat him on Friday, people will only say it was to be expected, seeing that Case rode in the Test and I didn't. That appears to give me an unfair advantage over Case which I would rather do without.

Smith contacted the Control Board to ask them why Tom had been left out and their reply was that they could give no reason. Smith said that this was the only sensible thing they had said during this whole episode because there was no reason. It wasn't just Smith and the New Cross faithful who were mystified. Even the national press took up the cudgels on Tom's behalf. The *Sunday People* said, 'Can anything be more ridiculous?' The *Daily Mail* added, 'Farndon's absence may easily cost the Home Country the match.' The *News Chronicle* said, 'A surprising feature [of the England team] is the omission of Tom Farndon, the Open Champion.'

Fred Mockford, writing in the New Cross programme said, 'I suppose I had better not say what I think about it, otherwise I shall be on the carpet, but I do feel very strongly that we are entitled to some explanation.' Mockford never did get his explanation, and why England's best rider was left out of the Test team was never made clear.

While all this was going on and Tom was getting ready for his British Championship challenge, New Cross took on Wimbledon at home. In the second heat of the match, Tom recorded a new track record time of 59.6 seconds. This was the first time the one minute mark had been beaten from a standing start on any track in the country and was yet another speedway landmark for Tom.

At last, on 5 and 7 June, Tom put his British Championship on the line. However, the competition turned into a bit of a farce; in the first leg at New Cross, Case fell in both races, giving Tom a 2–0 victory. In the second leg, two days later, at Hackney, the first race had to be started four times before they finally got away, only for Case to fall yet again, this time on the first bend. Tom was now just one race away from retaining his title, his opponent having fallen in all three races so far. However, in the second race of the second leg, Case managed to get away first and came out of the second bend in front with Tom hanging on just behind. On the first bend of the second lap, Tom tried to cut inside Case, clipped his rear wheel and was thrown headlong into the fence. This time it was Case who finished alone. In the deciding race, Tom once again

Tom shows off his young son, Roy, to his New Cross team mates.

Tom Farndon and Dick Case wheel to wheel in the British Individual Championship decider at Wembley on 27 June 1935.

fell at exactly the same spot and so Case levelled the series at 1–1, though in fact, it was more like a wrestling score with Tom having the advantage, three falls to two. In not one race had both riders finished.

The deciding round was held at Wembley on 27 June. Twenty-two coach loads of supporters, a record for away supporters at any track, travelled to the Empire Stadium to cheer on their hero. This time it was a much better contest. In the first race Case got a tremendous start and was a length up on Tom at the first bend. Tom tried to sweep round the outside of Case on the first and second bends but only managed to lose more ground to the Hackney man. However, he closed up on the back straight and got inside Case on the third bend. From then on he pulled away, winning by thirty yards and smashing the Wembley rolling start four-lap record by four-fifths of a second.

In the second race, Case again got away first and was half a wheel ahead as they reached the first bend, but Tom held the inside and passed Case coming into the back straight. On the second lap, Case made a do-or-die effort to pass Tom, flinging his bike into the bend at an acute angle in an effort to draw level. But he misjudged the slide by a fraction of an inch and, instead of shooting by Tom, slid gracefully to the ground, leaving Tom to come home alone and retain his British Individual title.

The year's Star Championship was run along different lines. At the suggestion of New Cross co-promoter Cecil Smith, in his other capacity of Secretary to the Control Board, twenty-four top riders were chosen to compete in qualifying rounds at all the National League tracks, with the top sixteen riders going through to the final, which would be held on the now classic 20-heat, five rides each formula. Naturally, Tom was one of the twenty-four chosen.

Still without any word of explanation, Tom was reinstated in the England team for the Second Test match, scoring 14 paid 15 points out of a possible 18, the highest scoring rider on either side. In his only non-scoring race he crossed the white line on the first bend of the second lap and was excluded. There is no doubt that, even with the elite of Australia and England riding, Tom was the best rider on show that night and only deepened the mystery as to why he had been left out of the First Test.

The Third Test saw Tom score 11 paid 13 with an engine failure while leading in one race. His two defeats came from an old rival of his, Bluey Wilkinson. Tom's partnership with Bill Kitchen in the Second and Third Tests was one of the deciding factors in England's victory in both.

Following the Third Test, Tom's next meeting was his defence of the London Riders' Championship at New Cross. The format for this meeting was 18 heats of three riders per heat with each rider racing three races and the top

Dick Case.

three scorers going through to the final. Tom had no difficulty in winning his three first-round races to find himself up against two other unbeaten riders, his own captain and track specialist Ron Johnson, and Hackney Wick's Wally Lloyd. The crowd were looking forward to a great race as all three riders had been on sparkling form during the meeting, but the race proved to be something of an anti-climax. Tom, drawn on the outside, took the lead at the first corner and never looked like being headed. His win meant that he became the first rider to win the London Riders' Championship two years in succession.

The following week, New Cross, who had drawn the short straw in the National Trophy first round, found themselves up against Belle Vue in the first leg. Tom's first ride was in Heat 2. He and his partner, George Newton,

The England team for the 1935 England v Australia Test match at New Cross. From left to right: Geoff Pymar, Tommy Croombs, Joe Abbott, Frank Charles, Bill Kitchen, Tom, Jack Parker, Eric Langton.

scored a 4–2, but it wasn't so much the 4–2 that sent the Old Kent Road crowd delirious as Tom's winning time of 58.4 seconds, an incredible 1.2 seconds faster than his own track record. During the four laps, Tom did not vary his course by more than a few inches. It was as near a perfect ride round the Frying Pan as you could ever hope to see. Going into the last heat, the scores were New Cross 49 Belle Vue 53. The same pairing was out in Heat 18. To stand any chance at all in the return leg, it was imperative that the New Cross riders even the match up with a 5–1. As the tapes rose, Tom got in front and literally hurled his bike into the first corner. He managed to emerge from the second bend just in the lead with his partner less than a length behind him and the Belle Vue pair less than a length behind him. The four riders raced the whole distance with no more than two lengths between first and last. But Tom not only held off the challenge, he was also able to shepherd Newton round for the much needed 5–1.

With the scores level, the pundits felt that the return was just a foregone conclusion and that the great Belle Vue side would have no trouble progressing to the next round. The away leg followed three days later on the hottest day of the year and it proved to be yet another memorable match. For most of this season and the season before, Belle Vue had seldom been extended on their own track, but this time New Cross took the fight to their opponents. Tom and Ron Johnson outrode their opponents, and by the halfway point, New Cross led by 7 points. Racing during the second half brought the home supporters to fever pitch as their team tried to overhaul New Cross. By the time the final heat came around the score was Belle Vue 52 New Cross 49. A 5–1 to New Cross would still give them victory, not only in this leg, but also overall. The atmosphere was electric and, as the riders came out onto the track, the noise was incredible as the cheering from both sets of supporters echoed around the stadium.

The New Cross pair was Tom and George Newton, while the whole of Manchester was relying on Joe Abbott and Acorn Dobson. It was Abbott who trapped first. In spite of a determined effort, Tom could find no way past. With Newton finishing in third place, the final score was Belle Vue 55 New Cross 52. Belle Vue were through, but thanks to Tom they knew they'd been in a fight.

Just after this, it was announced that Tom's next challenger for his British Title would be Belle Vue's Max Grosskreutz, the races to be held on 14 and 17 August. Meanwhile, Tom's initial appearance in the first round of the Star Riders' Championship came on his own track on 17 July. The format for these meetings was sixteen riders riding five times and meeting each other once over twenty heats. Tom finished with 12 points after his front wheel struck the boards in his third ride and he tumbled into the dust. The sixth and final round

Tom's young New Cross team mate, George Newton, who, like Tom, became one of the most spectacular riders of all time.

of the Star Championship qualifiers was held at West Ham on 13 August. After this the sixteen qualifiers were announced. Top was Bluey Wilkinson with 51 points. Tom was next on 48, one ahead of Jack Parker. Behind him came Dick Case and Max Grosskreutz on 45 and Ron Johnson on 43.

The first leg of Tom's defence of his British Championship took place the following night at New Cross. Inside running in the first heat gave Grosskreutz the lead going into the first bend after four false starts. He managed to keep Tom behind him for just about a lap and then Tom was through and away to win by 15 lengths. In the second heat, Grosskreutz turned into the first bend too acutely and fell, leaving Tom to finish the race alone and take a 1–0 lead.

The first race of the second leg saw Grosskreutz go into the lead again, but this time Tom overslid on the first bend and could never make up the lost ground and it was Grosskreutz's turn to win by 15 lengths. His time was 74.4 seconds, 1.2 seconds slower than Tom's four-lap rolling start record which he set at Belle Vue on 10 June. The first heat had shown Tom that his opponent's machine had a much higher gearing than his own so he decided on a slow approach to the starting line for the second heat. This resulted in a sequence of five false starts. Tom was then caught by surprise in the sixth attempt when, feeling certain that this was also a false start, he practically shut off only to find Grosskreutz enjoying the benefit of a 30-yard lead before he got going. He chased hard after Grosskreutz and by the end of the race had narrowed the gap to about four yards, but it has to be said that this was mainly due to Grosskreutz riding the last two laps on a flat tyre.

With the score standing at 1–1, the decider was held at Hackney Wick two nights later on 19 August. In the first heat, Grosskreutz took the lead from the start and rapidly established a big lead, winning as he liked in a new track record time of 68.4 seconds. Tom was now just one race away from losing his title, but he rose to the occasion magnificently as he had done countless times before. The second race was almost the reverse of the first with Tom well away and an easy victor.

As the rules stated, they tossed for position for the third run. Tom won and took the inside position but Grosskreutz was quick from the start and managed to get inside Tom on the first bend, streaking away down the back straight. With a typical Farndon effort, Tom burst through on the third bend and held his lead to the end of the first lap. From then on he increased it lap on lap to come home the winner and remain champion. His time was just .04 of a second slower than Grosskreutz's new track record. No rider in the history of the British Individual Championship had managed to retain the title after winning it. Tom had now beaten off four challengers and had proved himself master of the match race.

NEW CROSS SPEEDWAY
— TRACK RECORDS —

Four Laps.—Rolling Start
TOM FARNDON ... Time: 56.8 secs. ... Oct. 3rd, 1934

Four Laps.—Clutch Start
TOM FARNDON ... Time: 58.4 secs. ... July 10th, 1935

" The Ashes."—One Lap, Flying Start
TOM FARNDON ... Time: 14.2 secs. ... May 15th, 1935

Two-Lap Dash.—Rolling Start
TOM FARNDON ... Time: 29.6 secs. ... April 24th, 1935

INDIVIDUAL SCORE CHART

	RACE				TOTAL	
	1	2	3	4		
LIONEL VAN PRAAG (Captain)	2	2	3	2	9	THE WEMBLEY TEAM
GORDON BYERS ...	1	1	1		3	
FRANK CHARLES...	2	3	1	1	7	
JACK DIXON ...	0	0	2		2	
WALLY KILMISTER	2	2			4	
NORMAN EVANS ...	1	1	2	2	6	
DICKY SMYTHE (Reserve)	TOTAL				21	
RON JOHNSON (Captain)	3	3	3	3	12	THE NEW CROSS TEAM
ROY DOOK	0	-	-	-	0	
GEORGE NEWTON	1	0	1	1	3	
TOM FARNDON ...	3	3	3	3	12	
STAN GREATREX...	0	1	0	0	1	
JOE FRANCIS ...	3	2	2	3	10	
HARRY SHEPHERD (Reserve)	0	0	0	2	2	
	TOTAL				40	

8

A page from a 1935 New Cross programme showing that Tom held all the New Cross track records simultaneously.

Five nights after retaining the title Tom took his place in the England team for the final Test match against Australia. It was not a vintage performance from Tom, although he did score one spectacular victory over Bluey Wilkinson, taking him from behind and going on to win by 12 lengths. His final score was 10 points from six rides. This was Tom's last meeting before the fateful night of 28 August.

10

THE AFTERMATH

Posterity will know him, not only as the finest rider of all time, but as a traditional British Gentleman and Sportsman.

The day after Tom's death, which would have been Tom and Audrey's third wedding anniversary, New Cross were due to race at Wimbledon. Messrs Mockford and Smith proposed cancelling the meeting, but Audrey insisted it went ahead. 'Please carry on with the match,' she told the New Cross promoters. 'It would have been Tom's wish.' The Supporters' Club were due to have their annual outing to Dymchurch the following day as well, and again Audrey insisted it go ahead. Before the match at Wimbledon, 40,000 bare-headed supporters stood for a two-minute silence in honour of Tom.

The inquest on Tom's death was held at the Greenwich Coroner's Court on Tuesday 3 September in front of the Coroner, Dr Whitehouse. Thousands of people, including women with babies in their arms, crowded the narrow lane leading to the court. Audrey and her father, who had travelled down from Coventry, were among those present inside the court. Evidence was given by promoter Fred Mockford, mechanic Alf Cole, the steward on duty that night, Alfred Pickering, and the doctor, Dr C. Markby, who said that Tom had died from injuries to the brain although the skull itself was not fractured. The injuries, he said were consistent with a violent impact and not to being run over. He said that had Tom lived he would almost certainly have been unable to ride again. The jury returned a verdict of accidental death.

Two days later a memorial service, conducted by the Revd Mr J.B. Cowell of St James's, New Cross, was held at the stadium in front of 5,000 people, including the whole of the New Cross team and management. Many other riders, including Bluey Wilkinson, Vic Huxley, Tiger Stevenson and Arthur Atkinson, himself on crutches following a bad crash, were there. Tom's coffin was draped with the New Cross flag, orange with a black cross, and Tom's

In Loving Memory of
TOM FARNDON
(SPEEDWAY CHAMPION)
Age 24 Years
Who passed away after a crash at New Cross
Track, August 30th 1935
A Memorial Service will be held at
New Cross Track, Thursday 5th September 1935.
Loved by All Who knew Him
Interred at Coventry Cemetery 5/9/35

The invitation card to Tom's memorial service.

splintered helmet was placed on top. In front stood Tom's British Individual Championship trophy.

Audrey watched the service from the steward's box. At the service, the Revd Mr Cowell addressed the riders directly, saying, 'May I now say a word to the riders? It is this: You have suffered a sad and heavy blow, but for your old comrade's sake you must carry on with greater determination than ever. I know if he were here to speak to you he would say just these same words. He was the greatest of sportsmen, and his last words would be for you to carry on in the same way – sportsmen always.'

Tom's body was then taken by road for burial in his native Coventry. The coffin, still draped in the New Cross flag, halted at Willenhall before the procession went on to St Paul's Cemetery. Nearly 3,000 people were waiting outside while a further 1,000 were at the graveside including many of Tom's former riding colleagues from his Coventry days.

Tom's gravestone in Foleshill's St Paul's Cemetery is most remarkable and certainly the most unusual in the burial place. It was commissioned by Audrey and is an art deco depiction of a speeding motorcyclist in black marble carved by local sculptor, Richard Ormerod.

Some of the riders and officials at Tom's memorial service at New Cross stadium.
Back row, left to right: Geoff Pymar. Middle row: George Newton, Stan Greatrex,
Nobby Key, A.J. M. Ivison (Speedway Control Board), Ron Johnson, -?-, -?-. Front row:
Tiger Stevenson, Bluey Wilkinson, Maurice Stobart, Ken Brett, Arthur Atkinson,
Mick Murphy, Harry Shepherd.

It wasn't just New Cross which felt the loss. Supporters and riders from all
London teams were quick to express their sorrow at Tom's passing. On the
weekend after the funeral, hundreds of Wembley and Wimbledon supporters
made their way up to Coventry to visit Tom's grave to pay their respects.
The *Speedway News* published a number of letters from fans of other clubs.
A Harringay supporter wrote, 'I feel sure that all the Harringay supporters
would like to join with me in expressing our sincere regrets to the bereaved
wife of such a well-beloved champion, one who will never be forgotten.' A
Hackney Wick supporter added, 'May I be allowed to suggest the B.I.C. cup,
held by the late Tom Farndon, be presented to his widow as a mark of esteem
to show he died an undefeated champion?'

This idea was taken up by the West Ham team, who contacted all the
National League clubs asking them to join them in asking the ACU to
discontinue the British Individual Championship so as to perpetuate the

memory of Tom. This quickly gained support and the ACU readily agreed to the request. The New Cross management itself, of course, was not slow in making known its own tribute to Tom by announcing they were to hold a Tom Farndon Memorial Trophy meeting which would be contested every year in honour of their greatest rider.

At the first meeting at New Cross following Tom's death, Fred Mockford took to the microphone to pay tribute. He said:

We are gathered here tonight with an intense feeling of sadness in our hearts and under conditions which make the bond between us all very close and very intimate. The passing of Tom Farndon has removed from our midst one whom we can never replace, either as a rider or as a friend. As a rider his record needs no words of mine to extol – posterity will know him, not only as the finest rider of all time, but as a traditional British Gentleman and Sportsman. His interests were wrapped up in New Cross – not only on the track, the team or his fellow riders or management; he was the friend of the supporters as a whole. As you yourselves know, he was never too occupied to talk with you, to laugh with you and to share your personal thoughts, and many of you have enjoyed his advice and succour as we have ourselves. His personal charm was such that even when visiting other tracks as the most formidable rival to their own riders, he endeared himself to their supporters, and our tragic loss is little less to them as it is to us. In the midst of our own deep sorrow, our heartfelt sympathy and understanding are tendered to Mrs Tom Farndon and his family in their irreparable loss. Cut off at the height of his career, after having attained the goal he set out to reach, we remember him now, not for all he has done for the profession he chose, but for all he was himself, as a husband, a father, and a very good comrade and friend. Will you please stand for two minutes in silent tribute to the everlasting memory of Tom Farndon.

Two weeks later, the first Tom Farndon Memorial Trophy meeting was held. Fred Mockford and Cecil Smith wrote in the night's programme:

Who and what was this boy who captured the hearts of so many thousands of people wherever he went? Captured them, not for a little while, but decisively and permanently, holding them as surely as he held all the honours he won. The same sterling qualities which later caused the admirers of Tom Farndon to be numbered in thousands and his name to be known all over the world, took him into the Coventry team at the age of eighteen, seven short years ago. Those same qualities enabled

The scene at Tom's memorial service.

him to reach the peak of his profession, and then to hold it gracefully and with credit. Like most other boys, the spirit of adventure was strong in him, but it is easy to believe that to Tom Farndon the arduous path of adventure stretched ever before him, beckoning him on, but always reflecting the smile he seemed never to be without. He saw in Speedway Racing something which gave him an outlet for his boundless energy and vitality, and the few meetings he saw at the Brandon track in Coventry were sufficient to cause him to forsake the bench for the Speedway track.

From the start he commanded attention. His nature compelled him to put everything he knew into anything he attempted, and his dashing and wholehearted style made him always the centre of attraction. He came to London in 1931, and he arrived in his new team (then known as Crystal Palace) in the very midst of a period which is now history. Throughout

121

Mourners continued to gather at Tom's grave many years after he was killed. This photograph is from 1949 and shows the art deco memorial stone, a speeding motorcyclist in black marble, carved by local sculptor Richard Ormerod and commissioned by Tom's wife, Audrey.

the greater part of that year the whole mechanical side of the team was in a state of experiment, and Tom suffered from it as much as any other. But at the close of 1931 the Speedway world was electrified by the speed and reliability of the machines, which were faster and better than those of any other.

It is right from this time that the ascendancy of Tom Farndon can be dated. His style and his methods were such that the entirely new departure in machines can almost be said to have been made for him. Added to this was the fact that he had the necessary skill and courage to make use of the enormous power and speed of his motor.

In the following year he started on his record-breaking career, putting up new figures on almost every track he rode. His speed of 49.37 miles an hour on his own track was never equalled, and he stamped his name indelibly in the top flight of riders at the close of 1933 by winning the final of the Star Championship.

At the beginning of 1934 New Cross opened its gates, and in a few short weeks he completely eclipsed his earlier reputation. From his very first meeting he had weighed up the possibilities of the track and discovered the way in which it should be ridden. Again the mark of a Champion. But he did more than that. Speedway Racing was breaking new ground, taking the Sport to a new district, to a new crowd. Tom Farndon showed them Speedway Racing as only an expert can show it. He showed it them in his own style, which was unlike that of any other rider; he showed it them at its most spectacular and its most thrilling. And the people, although seeing something new, something they did not altogether understand, at once recognised in it the skill, the courage and the dashing sportsmanship of the boy they at once took to their hearts.

He came to New Cross the reigning Star Champion; in a few weeks he added to that the title of London Champion, which he won against the best riders in London. When, shortly afterwards, he was chosen as the challenger for the British Individual Championship, Tom Farndon saw his chance and he seized it with both hands. He smashed two records in beating the holder away, and lowered the record on his own track to 59 3/5 seconds, thereby becoming the first rider to cover a Speedway track in under one minute.

In the unique position of a Triple Champion his way became more arduous than ever. Every other first-class rider, in the true spirit of friendly rivalry, sought for and enjoyed a tilt at him, whether it was in the course of a Test Match or a Cup or League event. The result was that Tom Farndon was ever at the highest peak of endeavour and always riding as a Champion is expected to ride.

But he wore his honours lightheartedly, and his constant stream of new records showed that he rode without ever letting up. It is in this fact, rather than that he held one or more records on every track in the country, that he proved himself to be a Champion among Champions.

Four times he was called upon to defend his Individual Title against the best that could be found; four times he defended it successfully, retaining it longer than any other previous holder. He was undefeated to the end. Perhaps the most striking tribute to his skill and his scrupulous fairness is that in these victories he gained not only the goodwill and the approbation of all those who saw him, but that, also, of the losers themselves.

Tom Farndon won many races and he lost many. In victory he found no use for boasts or swagger; rather would he find a reason for the failure of the other. In defeat he was foremost among those who made no excuses.

He scorned to blame his machine or those responsible for it, and invariably put down his defeats to some error of judgment on his own part. Holding, as he did at one time or another, everything that Speedway had to offer, the idol of many thousands wherever he went, he remained the modest and unspoiled boy he was at the outset of his remarkable career.

Look around you, fellow spectators, at the man on your right, the woman on your left, and across the stadium in every direction; behind you; all those people have come, perhaps, straight from their workshops, their offices or their factories, charged with the same definite purpose as yourselves – to honour his memory and give practical support to those who he has left.

Later that evening, the Mayor of Lewisham, Councillor J.E. Pearson, presented the Tom Farndon Memorial Trophy to Belle Vue's Eric Langton, while all the proceeds of the evening went into the Tom Farndon Memorial Fund which had been set up for the benefit of Audrey and Roy. Cecil Smith said that while New Cross would have run a benefit meeting in any case, they were even more anxious to make the occasion an outstanding success because Tom's untimely death had prevented him from making adequate provision for his family in the way he would have wished. He added 'all speedway riders are commonly supposed to amass fabulous sums of money, and it must be admitted that in the early days some men did acquire small fortunes. Unfortunately, this does not apply in Farndon's case. He made the best of every available opportunity, but it should be remembered that his career as a star began long after the big money days had come to an end, and was of comparatively short duration.'

Tom's loss was a tragic blow to New Cross and knocked the stuffing out of the other riders and the fans. The rest of the season was meaningless and they lost every single one of their subsequent matches, falling from second in the league to one from bottom.

The following year, the last meeting of the season saw the second running of the Tom Farndon Memorial Trophy. The winner was New Cross's new star, Jack Milne. Although more than a year had elapsed since Farndon's death, his memory lived strongly in the hearts and minds of the supporters. Every Sunday small groups still travelled to Coventry to visit his grave to pay tribute to this great sportsman. The trophy was presented by Audrey and just for once the hard-bitten businessman, Fred Mockford, normally to be seen striding about the centre green in his fur coat barking out orders and whipping up the crowd, was so moved that he stood motionless almost in tears as Tom's widow handed the cup to Jack Milne.

When Tom's will was read on 5 December 1935, it was found he had left £2,166 18s to his widow, Edith Audrey Farndon and his father-in-law, Albert

Sid Farndon presents Belle Vue and England's Peter Craven with the 1959 Tom Farndon Memorial trophy.

Gledhill; a sum, which in today's money equates to £74,826.51. Audrey lived on the interest from the Memorial Fund and Tom's will for twenty-five years until 1960. The capital from the fund was to be held in trust until Roy reached the age of twenty-five under his grandfather's instructions. At this time the capital was to be split, with Roy receiving two-fifths and Audrey three-fifths. Roy married Betty and went to live in Malta in 1957, returning to this country when he was twenty-four. They managed to buy a house using the money they had saved while in Malta as a deposit. Roy then wrote to the Trustees asking if he could have his share of his father's memorial fund a year early because they needed to buy furniture for their new house. This was agreed and Roy received £300, which bought him and Betty a dining room suite, a bedroom suite and two fireside chairs. Audrey's share was £450. She died in 1974 at the age of sixty-two. Roy died in 2008 at the age of seventy-four.

11

WAS THE BEST YET TO COME?

If Tom Farndon had been idolised in the Thirties, his star could have shone with unimaginable brightness in the Fabulous Forties. By 1950 he would have been World Champion four times and the first speedway rider to win two world titles in succession. . . .

Tom Farndon had a unique and rare talent. It took him to the very pinnacle of his profession, and his dazzling achievements assuredly rank him among the very greatest the sporting world has had the privilege of being given from the art of speedway racing. The tragedy of Wednesday 28 August 1935 poses the question: Was the best of Tom Farndon yet to come?

His racing career was cut short when he was only twenty-four. He could, quite conceivably, have been in his prime when the incredible post-war boom thrust speedway racing before an audience of literally millions. If Tom Farndon had been idolised in the 1930s, his star could have shone with unimaginable brightness in the 'Fabulous Forties'.

At the age of thirty-five he would have been younger than most of the veteran maestros who took to the track again when league racing returned in 1946, the likes of his old Coventry captain Jack Parker, the northern Aces such as Eric Langton and Wally Lloyd, the southern stars such as Bill Kitchen and Tommy Price and his enduring Coventry team-mates Norman Parker and Bill Pitcher; not forgetting the Australian masters, of course: Ron Johnson, Lionel Van Praag and the explosively excellent Vic Duggan. Most of them who remained in England had kept their racing eye in at the wartime Saturday afternoon meetings at Belle Vue's old Hyde Road stadium. And no doubt Tom would have done the same.

A decade ago, in the edition of *Vintage Speedway* magazine for the Spring of 1999, John Chaplin expressed the opinion, 'Tom Farndon's destiny was surely

Tom 'had a unique and rare talent that took him to the very pinnacle of his profession.'

to be the greatest speedway rider England ever produced. His potential had appeared to be limitless.'

There is no reason to retract a word of that assessment. In fact, had he lived, Tom Farndon would have probably become the first speedway rider to win two World Championships in succession, 1936 and 1937, and, had there been no war, by 1950 he could have been the world title holder four times.

For what it's worth we are of the opinion that Bluey Wilkinson would still have won in 1938, and the 1939 Final, had it been allowed to take place, would have been won by America's Cordy Milne, with England's Arthur Atkinson second. However, Tom Farndon's achievements could well have even surpassed those of that other late great, Peter Craven.

There are some classic words once memorably and indelibly written by the finest speedway journalist of this or any other time, Basil Storey, editor in the early post-war years of the fabulously successful and influential *Speedway Gazette*. Basil wrote, 'Once in every generation in every sphere of sport a giant crosses the stage and leaves a memory which no successor can erase from the minds of those who witnessed the performance. Speedway racing is no exception.'

Basil might have been describing the influence of Tom Farndon, but he wrote those words a full twelve years after Tom's passing about another speedway phenomenon, Vic Duggan, who, throughout the 1947 season in Britain, had been, like Tom, almost unbeatable. How fittingly apposite the prose is when applied to the memory of Tom Farndon. For Basil also wrote, 'He has become a being apart . . . a living legend . . . it would be impossible for him to rise to greater heights. No man . . . in the history of the sport has more completely fulfilled a promise.'

Of course, there are those who question the Farndon aficionados' claim to the magnificence of his qualities. Only recently gentlemen (or could it have been ladies?) hiding behind a pseudonymous cloak of anonymity on the internet by calling themselves fastfire212 and raceleader (though invited to reveal their true identities, neither had the courage to do so) suggested that Tom did not ride against America's Jack and Cordy Milne and Wilbur Lamoreaux and therefore could not be considered the 'Best'. The theories are, of course, ludicrous, ill-thought-out and hypothetical. To attempt to minimise Tom's prowess because he never met the Milnes or Lammy on the track is as preposterous as dismissing his achievements because he didn't mix it with the likes of Price, Craven, Fundin, Briggs, Mauger, Olsen, Moore, Collins, Knutson, Gundersen, Michanek, Nielsen, Gollob, Rickardsson, Crump or Pedersen. One of the self-styled internet speedway experts said that Tom never competed outside the United Kingdom. Well, if he/she reads this book they will find out that he did – in New Zealand, and against some of the very best of his contemporary generation.

Tom leading George Wilks at Hackney.

It is, of course, a pointless exercise to begin comparing the top men of differing eras. For one thing, the average modern fan can see no further back than Ivan Mauger. Witness the poll conducted nine years ago by *Speedway Star* magazine in conjunction with the *Vintage Speedway* magazine to find 'The Millennium Man'. Ivan Mauger was voted top, Peter Craven scraped in at no. 10 and it was not until no. 18 that the first pre-war big name appeared: Jack Parker. Vic Duggan was no. 23, Ron Johnson did not turn up until no. 56 and Tom Farndon was at no. 57. Jack Milne was at no. 81.

Yet on the Old Time Speedway Forum, an internet discussion group, which conducted a recent poll to determine the top ten Greatest Of The 1930s, Tom Farndon won, polling almost twice the number of votes as his nearest rival, Jack Milne. The full list was:

1: Tom Farndon. 2: Jack Milne. 3: Eric Langton. Equal 4th: Bluey Wilkinson and Sprouts Elder. 6: Jack Parker. 7: Vic Huxley. 8: Wilbur Lamoreaux. 9: Jack Ormston. 10: Lionel Van Praag.

Of course, there are the other components which make comparisons futilely onerous: the differing track surfaces and machinery development and the fact that, indisputably, talent will rise to the top and the greats of any time would be great in whatever era of the sport they competed.

There is, naturally, a special aura about dead heroes and heroines, especially those who died in their youth. Duncan Edwards, the Manchester United football prodigy was one, as were Formula 1's Jim Clark, Piers Courage, Mike Hawthorn and Ayrton Senna; so were speedway's Norman Clay, Ken LeBreton, Frank Charles, Bluey Wilkinson, Simon Wigg, Tommy Jansson, Ray Duggan, Alan Hunt and Kenny Carter. Then there are actors such as James Dean and Marilyn Monroe, people like the revolutionary Che Guevara and President John F. Kennedy.

But it is not just the fact that they died young that has conveyed upon them what the world at large considers immortality, but their remarkable abilities and how they used them to achieve universal greatness in their fields.

Tom Farndon was a glamorous and charismatic figure, outstanding among his contemporaries, which is why he captured our imaginations many years ago and, as a speedway commentator and writer, inspired John Chaplin to not only try to discover what it was that made him so outstanding but, having seen the unique memorial to him in St Paul's Cemetery, to find and meet his family.

It did, out of necessity, take years, and several false trails, before John finally tracked down Tom's son Roy and his wife Betty to the Costa Blanca in Spain. It was in their palm- and orange tree-shaded garden beside their pool that he

Tom with Roy on the
bonnet of his Vauxhall
car.

actually held in his hand Tom's Star Championship medals and his Test match plaques. It was John's privilege to know them and observe their unassuming and modest pride in the adulation that has followed the legend of Tom Farndon to this very day.

They had no factual family record, other than their proud memories and the threadbare remains of the blue and gold sash Tom won at Monmore Green, Wolverhampton in 1929. The detailed record of Tom's career and life – and death – was lovingly compiled by Eric Dillon, and many of the illustrations he collected appear in these pages.

Though Tom is gone, he may not have been entirely lost to this world. It was reported quite recently that the ghost of Tom Farndon had been seen in the cemetery where he is buried. The report was posted on the internet by Lorraine Tedds. Her family are from Coventry but she now lives near Scarborough. She experienced the phenomenon and her account of the incident was this:

It must have been a Saturday when it happened, because we often went swimming in the summer months. My brothers Gary and Brian, a friend, Johnny Price and myself all decided that if we walked alongside the railway track we could get to the swimming pool just as quick as if we had taken the bus. But even better, the money we saved on bus fares could be used on extra sweets. On our way home we were busy making small talk, laughing and giggling, recalling events of that day's swim, when as we were walking on the part of the embankment that ran alongside St Paul's cemetery, we were stopped in our tracks by the loud noise of a motorbike engine coming from the cemetery. We turned to glance over at the graveyard and to our amazement saw a motorbike with a rider in the middle of the graveyard path revving and revving the motorbike; the rider was just revving and revving the bike while looking in our direction. I couldn't see his face clearly as he had a full face helmet on. The helmet, as far as my mind's eye recalls, was kind of metallic silver/blue, the rider was wearing all black and the motorbike was black, but a very shiny black which in the sunlight shone and glistened. As children we had never seen any motorbike or rider looking such as this, the only motorbikes and riders we had ever seen were always just plain black bikes with the rider having the 'Jerry' type helmet and goggles. So to see such a bike and rider as this was really scary. In our child minds we thought this must be one of those Hell's Angels that we had heard about but never seen. The image was very clear, it was a sunny afternoon around, I would think, 4 p.m. How long we stayed there mesmerised and glued to the spot I don't know, maybe only seconds but it seemed like ages. Suddenly the rider dropped his clutch and the bike started heading our way. Instantly we all just turned and ran as fast as we could, jumping over a barbed wire fence to get home even quicker. My brothers and I were all much taller than our friend Johnny and had no problem clearing the fence, but Johnny could not jump it and had to scramble on his hands and knees under the wire. We were too afraid to wait for him. My brothers and I continued running till we got home. We promised each other never to tell our parents because we would have been in trouble for walking alongside the railway and also for spending our bus money. That night in bed, because I was still scared, I told my sister Patricia all that had happened. Days later Johnny came round to see my brothers and told them that he had run home crying because while he was trying to get himself unstuck from the wire, he heard a smash and heard screaming, and he thought that the rider had got out of the cemetery and was coming to get him. A few days after the incident Patricia came home from school all excited and told me that they had a ghost story for the last lesson that day and the teacher told of a motorbike rider who was killed in a race and his motorbike was buried with him in St. Paul's Cemetery and that on the anniversary of his death, people had witnessed a bright light going around the graveyard and heard the sound of a motorbike. Was it the legendary Tom Farndon we saw? I do know that the image I saw was as clear and as solid looking as any living thing can be, yet it shined and glistened more brightly than anything I had ever seen before.

Lorraine went on to say that after discovering Tom's name, she scoured the internet to find out as much information about him as she possibly could, and said, 'I want to thank you and all the people like you who take the time to put pictures or information on the internet because, with your help, I have discovered just who my Ghost Rider really was, the great legendary Tom Farndon. May his soul rest in peace.'

Whatever the truth about Lorraine's remarkable experience, the legend of Tom Farndon lives on, permanently we hope with this appreciation of his life and career. Many have been the accolades heaped upon his memory, but we prefer this:

He was said to possess the perfect combination of skill, judgment and daring, he was utterly fearless and essentially an individualist intent on winning every race. He had amazing vitality and stamina and he typified the unquenchable spirit of adventurous youth . . .'

But you soon run out of superlatives when you try to do justice to Tom Farndon.

APPENDIX ONE

League Averages

Between 1929 and 1934 league matches were raced over nine heats with each rider having a maximum of three rides. However, to make meaningful comparisons with the way averages are calculated today we have assumed four rides per match to give a maximum of 12.00. In addition, in 1929 and 1933, winning riders were awarded four points. Again this has been converted to three for the purpose of giving a meaningful comparison.

Year	M	R	P	BP	TP	CMA	FMAX	PMAX
1929:	12	33	57	5	62	7.52	1	0*
1930:	22	66	134	3	137	8.30	4	0
1931:	34	97	152	13	165	6.80	4	1
1932:	33	99	195	5	200	8.08	4	1
1933:	34	100	232	7	239	9.56	9	1
1934:	32	96	240.5	1	241.5	10.06	14	1
1935:	19	76	182	3	185	9.74	5	1

*1929 incomplete = 12 out of 15 appearances.

APPENDIX TWO

Test Match Record

From 1933 onwards, Test matches were normally run over 18 heats with each rider programmed for six rides. For the purposes of the calculated match average (cma) and to give meaningful comparisons, we have used this formula so that the cma is based on six rides per match with the maximum possible therefore being 18.00.

1931
21 August, Third Test, Wembley: Reserve. 2 points from 2 rides.
23 September, Fifth Test, Stamford Bridge: Reserve. Did Not Ride
Overall CMA: 6.00

1932
4 June, First Test, Stamford Bridge: 11 + 1 points from 4 rides.
21 June, Second Test, Wembley: 0 points from 4 rides*.
16 July, Third Test, Belle Vue: 11 points from 4 rides.
6 August, Fourth Test, Crystal Palace: 2 + 1 points from 3 rides.
15 September, Fifth Test, Wembley: 7 +1 points from 4 rides.
Overall CMA: 10.73
*Two falls and two engine failures.

1933
29 June, First Test, Wembley: 1 point from 3 rides.
15 July, Second Test, Belle Vue: Reserve. 0 points from 2 rides.
29 July, Third Test, Crystal Palace: 11 points from 6 rides.
21 August, Fourth Test, Wimbledon: 11 + 1 points from 6 rides.
5 September, Fifth Test, West Ham: 10 points from 5 rides.
Overall CMA: 9.27

1934

7 June, First Test, Wembley: 8 points from 6 rides.
20 June, Second Test, New Cross: 9 + 2 points from 6 rides.
9 July, Third Test, Wimbledon: 4 + 3 points from 6 rides.
21 July, Fourth Test, Belle Vue: 4 + 1 points from 5 rides.
21 August, Fifth Test, West Ham: 7 + 1 points from 5 rides.
Overall CMA: 8.36

1935

19 June, Second Test, New Cross: 13 + 2 points from 6 rides.
6 July, Third Test, Belle Vue: 11 + 2 points from 6 rides.
30 July, Fourth Test, West Ham: 6 + 1 points from 5 rides.
24 August, Fifth Test, Harringay: 10 + 4 points from 6 rides.
Overall CMA: 12.78

Overall Test CMA: 10.09

APPENDIX THREE

British Individual Championship

1932 – Challengers' Competition

First Round

23 April, Crystal Palace:	Tom Farndon 2	Colin Watson 0
5 May, Wembley:	Tom Farndon 2	Colin Watson 0
Overall:	Tom Farndon 2	Colin Watson 0

Semi-Final

11 June, Stamford Bridge:	Tom Farndon 2	Frank Arthur 1
18 June, Crystal Palace:	Tom Farndon 1	Frank Arthur 2
21 June, Plymouth:	Tom Farndon 1	Frank Arthur 2
Overall:	Tom Farndon 1	Frank Arthur 2

1934 – Championship

30 July, Wimbledon:	Tom Farndon 2	Vic Huxley 0
1 August, New Cross:	Tom Farndon 2	Vic Huxley 0
Overall:	Tom Farndon 2	Vic Huxley 0
5 September, New Cross:	Tom Farndon 2	Ron Johnson 0
Overall:	Tom Farndon 1	Ron Johnson 0
3 October, New Cross:	Tom Farndon 2	Max Grosskreutz 1
6 October, Belle Vue:	Tom Farndon 1	Max Grosskreutz 2
11 October, Wembley:	Tom Farndon 2	Max Grosskreutz 1
Overall:	Tom Farndon 2	Max Grosskreutz 1

1935 – Championship

5 June, New Cross:	Tom Farndon 2	Dick Case 0
7 June, Hackney Wick:	Tom Farndon 1	Dick Case 2
27 June, Wembley:	Tom Farndon 2	Dick Case 0
Overall:	Tom Farndon 2	Dick Case 1

14 August, New Cross:	Tom Farndon 2	Max Grosskreutz 0
17 August, Belle Vue:	Tom Farndon 0	Max Grosskreutz 2
19 August, Hackney Wick:	Tom Farndon 2	Max Grosskreutz 1
Overall:	Tom Farndon 2	Max Grosskreutz 1

After Bluey Wilkinson had been chosen as Tom's next challenger, Tom was involved in his fatal accident. As a mark of respect the competition was abandoned to perpetuate Tom's name as the unbeaten holder of the trophy.

APPENDIX FOUR

Tom Farndon Memorial Trophy

Winners

1935:	Eric Langton (Belle Vue)
1936:	Jack Milne (New Cross)
1937:	George Newton (New Cross)
1938:	Bluey Wilkinson (West Ham)
1939–45:	Not Held
1946:	Malcolm Craven (West Ham)
1947:	Jeff Lloyd (New Cross)
1948:	Howdy Byford (West Ham)
1949:	Wilbur Lamoreaux (Birmingham)
1950:	Graham Warren (Birmingham)
1951:	Jack Young (Edinburgh)
1952–8:	Not Held
1959:	Peter Craven (Belle Vue)
1960:	Ronnie Moore (Wimbledon)
1961:	Jack Young (Coventry)

ACKNOWLEDGMENTS

First and foremost the authors would like to thank the Farndon family for all their help and cooperation in the writing of this book. Tom's daughter-in-law, Betty, has been a mine of information and has kindly allowed us access to the Farndon family archives including their photographs and scrapbooks, three of which were compiled by devoted Tom Farndon fan, Eric Dillon. She has also kindly written the foreword for this book. Much background family information came from Tom's son, the late Roy Farndon, and sister, the late Hilda Haden, much of which was reproduced in a two-part series written by John Chaplin and published in *Vintage Speedway Magazine*, Vol. 7 Nos 1 & 2, Spring and Summer 1999.

In addition the following have been of great help in providing factual and statistical information: Nigel Bird, Peter Jackson, Barry Stephenson, Ross Garrigan, Terry Stone and Keith Green as well as the Speedway Researcher website: http://www.speedwayresearcher.org.uk. Our thanks to all of them.

All photographs are the property of the Farndon family, the authors, Mike Kemp and John Somerville who have kindly allowed us to reproduce them.

Other titles published by The History Press

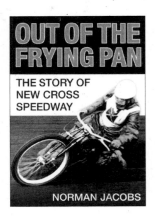

Out of the Frying Pan
The Story of New Cross Speedway
Norman Jacobs
978-07524-4476-5
Paperback

Written by respected speedway historian Norman Jacobs, this book tells the story of each season, from the inaugural 1934 campaign, through the post-war years and the New Cross revival after a temporary hiatus in the 1950s up until the track's closure in 1963.

Ove Fundin: Speedway Superstar
John Chaplin
978-07524-2944-1
Paperback

John Chaplin's book discusses the life and career of Ove Fundin, perhaps the greatest speedway champion of all time, who won the world title 5 times during the 1950s and 1960s. Well-researched and including exclusive interviews with family, friends, and competitors, this book is necessary reading for all speedway fans.

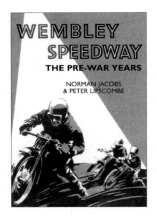

Wembley Speedway: The Pre-War Years
Norman Jacobs & Peter Lipscombe
978-07524-3750-7
Paperback

In 1929 when the Empire Stadium took up speedway, with Sir Arthur Elvin – 'Mr Wembley' – at the helm, it gave the sport (then new to Great Britain) an air of respectability and helped bring it into the mainstream. The first 'big name' in British speedway, the Wembley Lions enjoyed early success and then went on to win seven out of eight league titles between 1946 and 1953.

Visit our website and discover thousands of other History Press books.
www.thehistorypress.co.uk